THREE PLAYS
BY ADRIANO SHAPLIN

Adriano Shaplin

THREE PLAYS

WRECK THE AIRLINE BARRIER
VICTORY AT THE DIRT PALACE
PUGILIST SPECIALIST

OBERON BOOKS
LONDON

First published in this collection in 2004 by Oberon Books Ltd
521 Caledonian Road, London N7 9RH
Tel: 020 7607 3637 / Fax: 020 7607 3629
e-mail: oberon.books@btinternet.com
www.oberonbooks.com

A catalogue record for this book is available from the British
Library.

ISBN: 1 84002 489 5

Printed in Great Britain by Antony Rowe Ltd, Chippenham.

Contents

Notes on these plays in performance

All of the texts within this volume were written for, and originally performed by, the Riot Group. In each case, roles were written with specific company members in mind. In *Wreck the Airline Barrier*, I just used the actor's first initial in the text. Stage directions were used infrequently and inconsistently because I did not, at the time, have any 'readers' in mind other than the company. In some places I have added stage directions to explain to a reader what happened in our performance.

The Riot Group have developed a kind of directing and design style which informs these pieces a great deal. Settings tend to be ill-defined or fluid. Sets are minimal. Space, time, and sometimes character tend to be suggested more by light, sound, and actor-focus than by any concrete material. All actors occupy the stage at all times and generally face the audience while speaking. In short, a whole range of self-imposed restrictions, rules, and stylistic fanaticisms govern the creation of each Riot Group production, and these 'choices' are reenforced by, and deeply embedded within, each text.

In publishing these scripts I allow that they can be interpreted for the stage in many ways, and maybe even enjoyed as bits of writing on their own. At the same time, the context in which they were originally written and performed – as part of a tight-knit ensemble with a fairly rigid aesthetic prerogative – seems important to mention.

WRECK THE AIRLINE BARRIER

Characters

STEVE SALVON

STONE SALVON

SARAH SALVON

STEWARDESSES, PILOTS, 'WITCHES', VOICES
played by members of the cast

Notes on production

In *Wreck the Airline Barrier* three motivational speakers wake up, drive to an airport, meet each other, board a plane, then die when the plane crashes. Throughout the play they are interrupted by stewardesses, pilots, 'witches', voices from beyond, and voices inside their heads. The play is written so that all roles are divided among the three actors. I have given a rough indication of who the actors are playing at the top of each scene. Slash marks (/) indicate interruption and overlapping.

Wreck the Airline Barrier, a Riot Group production, was first performed at Sarah Lawrence College in February 1999, and subsequently opened at the Edinburgh Fringe Festival on August 9, 1999. The cast was as follows:

D (Steve Salvon, Witch, Airline Staff), Drew Friedman

A (Stone Salvon, Witch, Airline Staff), Adriano Shaplin

S (Sarah Salvon, Witch, Airline Staff), Stephanie Viola

Directed and designed by The Riot Group

Sound by Adriano Shaplin

Stage Managed by Maria Shaplin

In August 1999 *Wreck the Airline Barrier* received the Scotsman Fringe First Award and the Herald Devil Award.

WRECK THE AIRLINE BARRIER

1

Witches:

D: Hey Salvon.

S: Yes Salvon.

D: Night is falling.

   Pause.

S: I know I can see it.

A: I can't sleep.

D: Salvon.

A: I think about birds.

S: Salvon.

A: And insects. And planes.

S: Salvon.

D: Night is falling.

   Pause.

S: I know I can see it.

   Pause.

A: I can't sleep.

S: I'll tell you a story.

A: That would help.

S: Once upon a time you can't teach an old dog new tricks.
   He had his cake and he ate it too. If it looks like a duck,

and quacks like a duck, and smells like a duck, it's probably a duck. Welcome to your life.

A: I don't feel any better.

Pause.

S: Salvon?

D: Yes sister?

S: Do we fly home tomorrow?

D: Yes sister.

S: I'm scared.

D: Salvon.

2

Steve, Stone and Sarah:

D: No. Thank you for calling. I slept well. It was cold but my blankets were warm. I'm packed. I dreamt about a wedding where everyone wore red. It was like a slaughter house.

S: No. That's fine. No, its always a pleasure to hear your voice. I'm up. I feel good today. I dreamt I saw a missile, launched in 1988, travel across the sky, but the sky wasn't clouds and blue space, it was television pixels.

A: No. I'm awake. No, I slept like a log. I'm ready to go. All packed. No, around her neck. I dreamt I knew you when you were fourteen, and my tongue in your ear. Now I'm wiping my eyes.

D: No, I plan on arriving an hour and a half early so I can confirm my ticket. I'm going to shower, shave, and probably eat at the airport. I packed very light. You'd be proud of me.

S: No. The airline says you should arrive an hour before your plane leaves to confirm your ticket. I set my alarm for seven a.m., I plan to arrive at the airport by eight-thirty. Between seven-fifteen and seven-thirty I'll take my shower.

A: I plan on showering by seven o'clock. I think it's important to get a good shower before you fly. When I fly my feet swell up and the hair on my feet gets that tight, itchy feeling. I try to avoid that.

D: I cherish these little moments of quiet. I've got no time for romance. I just run and run. Sometimes fly.

S: No, this is the last time I plan on flying without being afraid.

A: How are the numbers today? No, the numbers. How are the numbers? Could you fax me a reading on the numbers? Could you please call me on my 'cell phone'? Could you 'e-*mail*' the numbers this morning? Could you photocopy a document which describes the status of the numbers? / How are the numbers today?

D: How are the numbers today? No, the numbers. That bad? That's too bad. How are the bad?

S: The what?

D: The numbers, excuse me, how are the numbers?

S: Bad. They're that bad? How is that? Could you fax me the read-out? Well, then could you please transfer an electric color chart? Could you cross-reference the numbers? Perhaps while I'm flying you could send up a few smoke signals?

A: I'm not sure I understand: Agnostic? Oh. I thought you said 'agnostic'.

D: No, I'm just trying to get a fix on what you're feeding me here. You know. I'm processing the information. Yes. I'm just waking up here.

S: No, I slept all night. No. I'm fine. No, really, I'm fine. / Really.

A: Really? That's unusual. / Agnostic.

D: Agnostic? Oh, I thought you said 'agnostic'. No, I don't think that has anything to do with what we're talking about. No. It's just / what I thought you said.

S: That's what I thought you said. No, I'm not afraid. Afraid? No, I'm not. I'm not afraid to fly. / I'm not afraid to fly.

A: I'm not afraid to fly. I'm an agnostic. No, you said it. No I'm not saying that. Well, I guess that's / chicken or the egg.

D: Chicken or the egg. No I actually don't see what that has to do with what we're talking about. Actually, to be honest with you Salvon I've got to be going. / I've got a plane to catch.

S: I've got a plane to catch. No, that's fine. It's always a pleasure to talk to you. It's always a pleasure to hear the sound of your voice. You know, I've been meaning to tell you you have a very interesting voice. It's very interesting. I've often thought to myself: Someday you should just open up and tell him he has an attractive voice. You should just be honest and let him know that listening to his voice brings you a great deal of pleasure in the morning. What I'm trying to say is:

S / D: I don't think people are honest with each other enough. Just think: What would this world be like if people were just honest with each other? What would it be like? How would it feel, you know? Like, for example: I just told you I thought you had an attractive voice, and you seemed to respond positively to that.

S / D / A: In other words, being honest is the best policy. I didn't think, I acted. And that's what's important. Being honest. That's what's important, think about the social ramifications. A reorganization of society. Our problem, as people, is that we allow ourselves to be repressed by all sorts of fear and anxiety. We need to realize that the heart is not satisfied by dissatisfaction. That may sound like circular logic, but when you think about it, logic is circular. So I'm right about everything.

D: In conclusion, I'd like to say that honesty is the best policy. And things like lying and contradicting yourself are wrong. I'd also like to say that I think it's important to be true to yourself. And follow your dreams.

A: Life is a journey. It's a long journey, and you have to dive in and swim or you'll be in trouble, you'll be in a lot of trouble. If you don't swim, you sink. And if you sink, then you're not happy, and you're not being honest with yourself. And / the Heart Is Not Satisfied With Dissatisfaction.

S: The Heart Is Not Satisfied With Dissatisfaction. And in conclusion I'd like to say that self-confidence is key. You need to follow your dreams. 'Cause if you don't follow those dreams / they die.

A: They die. Like a fish that forgets how to swim, and sinks beneath the cool, clear water.

S: Don't be the chicken. Be the egg. Be the shell, which is hard and protective, but when life comes knocking, it's willing to crack.

A: Crack. Like, say, the bones of a child too weak to swim in the stream called / life.

D: Life is what you make of it. And your life is the only one you've got. Unless you believe in reincarnation. But even if you do, this is the only life you've got right now, and you have to live it to its fullest. 'Cause / this isn't a free ride.

S: This isn't a free ride. No one said it was going to be easy. 'Cause you've come to a fork in the road. / One path goes east. / The other goes west.

A: One path goes east.

D: The other goes west.

S: And one path is the path least traveled. The other is a FUCKING FIRESTORM OF HATE AND JEALOUSY.

D: BURNING IN A PIT OF FLAMES CALLED 'REGRET' AND 'INNER TORMENT'.

A: BELIEVING IN EMPTY WORDS AND EMPTIER GODS WHOSE PURPOSE IS TO CONTROL AND FUCKING MANIPULATE YOU.

S: DON'T BE FUCKING MANIPULATED. YOU HAVE A CHOICE. LIFE IS WHAT YOU FUCKING MAKE OF IT.

D: NOT WHAT YOUR STUPID FATHER TELLS YOU.

A: OR YOUR STUPID GRANDMOTHER.

S: OR ANY OF THOSE STUPID FUCKING IDIOTS.

D: THEY DON'T CARE ABOUT YOU. THEY ONLY CARE ABOUT THEMSELVES.

A: DON'T BE A FUCKING SLAVE.

S: STAND UP FOR YOURSELF YOU STUPID FUCKING IDIOT, YOU DON'T KNOW WHAT'S GOOD FOR YOU.

A: I've got to catch a plane.

D: Jesus what time is it.

S: I'm gonna hop in the shower.

Pause.

D: Hello. No I'm on my way to the airport. I'm in my car right now.

S: Yes. I just passed that sign. Yes, I'm making good time. The shower was perfect.

A: Uh huh. Yeah, I'll be there in two seconds okay. No, I'm making good time.

D: Okay, I really shouldn't be talking on the phone while I'm driving.

S: I'll call you when I get there. When I land. I'll call you. Six o'clock your time.

A: Think about me. I'll be thinking about you. Yes I will. I'm thinking about you right now.

D: I'm pulling up to the airport now. Yes. I'll see you soon.

S: Call me before you go to bed. Call me. And tell her I love her.

D: I love you sweetheart. Yes I do. I didn't even know what I wanted until I met you.

A: You may not be the smartest, or the prettiest, or the most attractive girl, but you're who I want to be with. Okay honey?

S: Tell her I love her, and tell her I'll bring her something back from Spain. Tell her to sleep tight. Yes I love you too. You complete me.

D: I better get off the phone now. I'm at the airport.

A: No, I dreamt that I knew you when you were fourteen, and my tongue in your ear. And my tongue in your ear. No, 'and my tongue in your ear'. I DREAMT THAT I KNEW YOU WHEN YOU WERE FOURTEEN AND MY TONGUE IN YOUR EAR. No, it's the connection. THE CONNECTION. My *tongue* in your *ear!* CLEAN

OUT YOUR FUCKING EARS YOU STUPID BITCH! YES! THAT'S RIGHT! Oh, you heard *that?* OKAY THEN. I LOVE YOU. TAKE CARE.

S: Yes, I'd like to confirm my ticket.

D: Okay, what's your name?

S: Sarah.

D: Last name.

S: Salvon.

D: And what is something that people notice about you that is special?

S: I've got nice boobs.

D: Something else?

S: I'm a good listener.

D: Okay, ticket confirmed.

A: Yes, I'd like to confirm my ticket.

S: Okay, what's your name?

A: Stone.

S: Stone what?

A: Salvon.

S: And what is something special about you that people tend to notice?

A: I'm cruel.

S: You're what?

A: I'm very cruel.

S: And something else?

A: I could give a shit.

S: About?

A: Anything.

S: Okay, ticket confirmed.

D: Uh, yes, I'd like to confirm my ticket.

A: I could give a shit.

D: Steve.

A: And your last name Steve?

D: Salvon.

A: Where are you flying today?

D: Spain. And... Spain.

A: And what is something that people notice about you which is special?

D: I'm tall.

A: You're tall.

D: And I'm commanding.

A: What else?

D: I have a positive mental attitude.

A: Great.

D: And I fuck really hard.

A: Spectacular. Ticket confirmed.

D: Actually I have a few questions.

S: Don't misunderstand me, I'm not scared to fly, but...

A: Where is the best place to sit on the plane, front middle or back?

D: What are the survival percentages for commercial air travel?

S: When a plane experiences a sudden decrease in cabin pressure, what percentage of the passengers are sucked out of the plane?

A: When was the last time this plane was inspected?

D: Are we going to be flying with an experienced pilot?

S: If something were to happen to the pilot, would the co-pilot be able to fly the plane?

A: If something were to happen to the co-pilot, would the stewardess be able to fly the plane?

D: If something were to happen to the stewardess, would I be able to fly the plane?

S: If I see a loved one die in front of me is it worth it to try and survive?

A: If I jump at the moment of impact will I fall into heaven?

D: If we crash into the ocean will the plane float or sink?

S: If I promise the plane my heart will it stay with me forever?

A: If I buy the plane a few drinks do you think it will go to bed with me?

D: If I come before the plane does should I make sure the plane gets off too or is that too pushy for a first date?

S: If I think about crashing will it make the plane crash?

A: If I think about crashing will it make the plane crash?

D: If thinking about crashing makes the plane crash how can I think about something else?

S: Am I the only one who thinks about crashing?

A: Is crashing something we are or something we do?

D: Are we keeping the plane up with collective karma?

S: Is the scientific study of flight an exercise in fiction?

A: Is it exhilarating to feel your body being torn apart at the moment of impact?

D: What if I say 'Macbeth' before our first performance?

S: At what point do you realize that your injuries are fatal?

A: That there will be no time to repair you before you die?

D: Why do plane crash victims call out the name of their worst enemy before they die?

A: Yeah, why do plane crash victims call out the name of their worst enemy before they die?

S: Well. I'll have the answer to these and more questions on the plane.

A: No, tell me now.

S: I can't answer those questions at this time.

A: No, tell me now.

S: Those are stupid questions.

A: They are not stupid questions.

3

Stone:

A: Those are not stupid questions. I get very scared. I'm very scared to fly, those are absolutely not stupid questions.

S / D: (*Whispered continuously throughout monologue but out of sync with each other.*) Then my heart breaks. / I can't help it. Life is dangerous. You grow up. No problem. Then something changes. I get scared. Then my heart breaks. I

can't help it. Life is dangerous. You grow up. No
problem. Then something changes. I get scared. Then
my heart breaks. I can't help it....

A: I get scared. I'm scared that we're going to crash. I think
I'm going to comb my hair. There that's better. Do you
have a magazine I could read? Thank you very much. I
think I'm going to comb my hair. There that's better. It's
like being naked up here. I can't help it. Life is
dangerous sometimes. Could you please stop breathing
on me? Please Salvon, deliver me safely. I don't deserve
this. I think I'm going to comb my hair. There that's
better. Does any one have a mint? Okay. Okay. It's much
safer in my mother's vagina. I dreamt I knew you when
you were fourteen and my tongue in your ear. It's a nice
thought. This magazine is really boring. I think I'm
going to comb my hair. That's better. God, I've been
here before. We're going down, we're going down, we're
going down. WHAT WAS THAT MY STOMACH?
Salvon, I rejoice in your heavenly power. You are greater
than I, more powerful than I. Say it over and over. I am
invincible in my conviction. I've seen my death, I was
there, I was skiing, I was supposed to die but that dog
with the hot chocolate saved me, made me invisible.
Now I'm going to live forever. I think I'm going to live
forever I think I'm going to comb my hair that's
BETTER. Salvon, okay okay, I can't help it. The oceans
boil I know they do please just humiliate me. I need to
eat dirt so I won't deserve to die. I think I'm going to
comb my hair. That's better. I've been here before. I
going to die in this fucking plastic fire-trap. Please just
cripple me with cancer or limblessness. Give me some
disease to struggle through. A broken neck. Diving
accident. Please, just don't punish me for being alive.
Make me blind. Even burns, I'll take burns. I just don't
want to be another anonymous white plane crash victim.
Some kind of quota for all the poor and unfortunates.
Some kind of sacrificial WEISS could you please stop

breathing on me? I didn't put any one in the ovens.
Please I'll take baldness or impotence, just not some
minor character status. Could you please stop breathing
on me?! Lung disease. Feel sorry for me, NOT HOW IT
IS NOW. I'm so dead I think I'm going to comb my
hair, that's better I know it's coming so fuck you all
YOU I'm sick of your whining. Bring it on. Split me you
fucking bloodsuckers. Fucking cunts. Fucking niggers.
Fucking teenagers. I bought you a dozen roses why don't
you choke on them you fucking faggots. I'll take a few of
you out with me for old times' sake the good old days
when your heads cracked the pavement. I can't help it.
Life is dangerous. You grow up. No problem. Then
something changes. I get scared. Then my heart breaks.

S: I can't answer those questions at this time.

4

Steve, Stone Sarah:

S: (*Intercom voice.*) Boarding will occur in ten minutes.
   Salvon!!

D: Well I guess I'll go / sit over here.

A: This seems like a good place to / sit down and relax.

S: I guess I'll sit over here and just read my magazine or
   maybe squeeze my thighs together over and over.

D: Yup. Just sitting here. Thinking.

A: Sure is nice in airports. I like them. Pretty great.

S: An airport is a place from which one only departs.
   Interesting.

D: An airport is not a place in and of itself. It is the sum
   total of numerous destinations. Interesting.

A: I wonder what that chick looks like naked?

S: I wonder if black men want to sleep with me and 'conquer the white princess'. I bet they do.

D: Hitler was a neat guy. I mean, everything he believed in was wrong, but he really believed in something.

A: I wonder if Hitler slept in his uniform.

S: I bet there would be something exciting about having sex in a concentration camp.

D: Did I turn off the stove?

A: Deformed people want me to look at them. They don't want me to look away. They want me to embrace and accept their deformity. They want me to look right at it. And stare. To show that I'm not afraid.

S: Also: midgets.

D: Also: really fat people.

A: Also: rich people.

S: If I didn't pay attention to midgets: who would?

D: Girls dream about being raped. I read all about that. Girls dream about it all the time.

A: Did I turn off the stove?

S: I think I'm getting my period.

D: I hope I get an aisle seat.

A: I wonder if that chick would fuck me as the plane crashed down?

S: Why is that guy staring at me?

D: While I'm waiting, I should review my notes towards a more complete self.

A: While I'm waiting I should do my positive meditation.

S: Okay Sarah, get focused. Get focused.

D: Rule Number One: All the guns are loaded with blanks.

A: Rule Number Two: It doesn't matter who pulls the trigger.

S: Rule Number Three: Animals are people too.

D: Rule Number Four: These are the sounds of the New York Underground.

A: Rule Number Five: It's only subliminal if you aren't listening.

S: Rule Number Six: Anyone can be trained to write with their right hand.

D: Rule Number Seven: Everyone has a different idea of what constitutes a good conversation.

A: Rule Number Eight: You have to earn your close-up.

S: God that's nice.

D: The Heart Is Not Satisfied By Dissatisfaction.

A: I know that it's true, but what about faggots?

S: (*Intercom voice.*) Boarding will occur in five minutes. Salvon!

D: Well, here it goes. Hey, my name's Steve.

S: My name is Sarah / Nice to meet you.

A: Nice to meet you, my name is Stone, I noticed you two talking and I thought I'd introduce myself I hope you don't / mind.

S: Mind? Nooo, God forbid. / The more the merrier.

D: The more the merrier. I taught my five-year-old son that phrase and now he says it all the time / isn't that something?

A: Isn't that something? You have children? It's funny you should mention it because / I have children, two of them.

S: I have children, two of them, one is six, the other is seven. I call them Samantha and / Steve.

D: Steve? that's my name, what a coincidence, my son's name is / Stick.

A: Stick? My name is Stone. That is the funniest thing I've ever heard! / Sticks and stones can break my bones / but words can never hurt me.

S: Sticks and stones can break my bones / but words can never hurts me.

D: But words can never hurt me.

A: I tell my son to say that whenever anyone calls him a nigger.

S: A nigger? But you're / white?

A: White? I know. All the kids call each other nigger nowadays, don't ask me, I don't get it, I just hope he doesn't get his feelings hurt.

Pause.

D: So, Sarah, where are you headed?

S: / Spain.

A: Spain? Are you serious? / Me too!

D: ME TOO!!!

S: (*Intercom voice.*) Attention, all passengers flying to Spain you may now board the plane. Salvon!

D / A: This is very exciting.

S: Yes it is.

D: It's nice to make new friends.

A: It's always nice to make new friends.

S: You guys are the best.

D: So, do you guys like Hitler?

A: Absolutely.

S: I've always loved Hitler.

D: I mean apart from the genocide.

S / A: Oh course!!!

A: What do you take me for?

S: You know, it's funny you bring him up because this morning, before I got to the airport I took a shower. Now, I know there is nothing special about that, after all I take showers all the time, but this morning something was different. I was a bit disorientated and, low and behold, I got soap in my eyes. I rarely ever do this, but today, I got soap all up in my eyes, as it were. God, how it burned. But you know what I did? I just thought: 'Sarah, at least you're not in a concentration camp.' And you know what? The pain went away.

5

Captain:

D: COME NEAR! Salvon! COME NEAR! Salvon! Please watch your step! Come in! Come near! Stand up! Stand up! This is your captain speaking! I want you to bring with you your positive energy, your Salvon, your trust in God, your faith in friendship and the magnetic bond you share with the earth! I want you to fill the cabin with safety-flavored good luck, individually wrapped confidence! Come near! There are peanuts, salty, salty peanuts, Bloody Marys and complimentary soda; a smorgasbord of lively, enriching, positive vibe entertainment! Come NEAR! Watch your step Salvon, Salvon, Salvon! Imagine Noah and the Ark! You march forward and with you you bring your pride, your earthly and unearthly pride, your belief that a safe landing is not

just good luck, it is the glorious will of God, it the
continuation of the species, it is REPRODUCTION, the
quantum mechanics of natural selection! Come NEAR!
My mouth is the red roof of the circus tent SALVON!
My teeth are the trapeze. My tongue: the last pair of
elephants! YOU: THE LAST PAIR OF ELEPHANTS!
Marching marching marching oh Lord Jesus someone
put lemonade in my lemonade Salvon! Children, come
near! These wings are the out-stretched arms of God,
Salvon, this is your pilot speaking, Salvon, the tail is a
force of nature GONG! The nose: a constellation of
mind-melting machinery, come near, come near! My
voice your passport! My voice is your passport! Let's
hear it for the lifeguards, the waitresses, the stewardesses,
the machine gunners, the cafeteria workers, the soldiers,
the animals and the ants marching two by two! Let's hear
it for all the college students, all the intellectuals and
political rabble-rousers. Lets hear it for all the hard-
working racists, the enduring Klan. Let's hear it for little
Mary Margaret and her tight snatch! Let's hear for the
Rocket Men, they all fly high! If niggers can do it so can
you!! If I can do it so can you!!! Come near, come near,
SALVON!!!! Come near, ladies and germs, this is the
final call for boarding, we are taxiing forward, let Salvon
extend his hand and bless our vessel, our flying firetrap,
a bubble of faith so unbreakable it must have been blown
by the devil. This is your final call, come near, come
near, Salvon, stand up and cheer! We are Noah's jet
plane, don't know when we'll be back again! The doors
are closing, it's chicken or the egg time, ladies and
germs. The doors are closing, the doors are closing,
Salvon! Let's get it on!

The plane takes off.

6

Airline Staff:

S: Good evening Salvon. I hope you all had a pleasant take-off. The plentiful food carts will be around shortly. Right now, we ask that all our passenger take a series of Rorschach tests before we reach full altitude. If you'll please plug your headphones into the jack on your right side armrest and direct your eyes towards me. Reply with one word only. Just speak out loud in a normal voice.

A: / Okay, that's an insect. Bird. Insects. Some kind of insect. that's also a bird. Vampire bat. Insect. Insect. Insects. Genitalia. Bird. Bat. Insect. Insect. Bird. Plane. Snowflake. I'm going to go with bird on that one. that's an insect. Insect. Bird. That one is either a plane, or an insect. Genitalia. Bird. Insect. Bird.

D: Okay, that's a bird, I think. Bird. Bird. That's a bird. That's a plane. That's a bat. Bird. Bird. Insect. That's also an insect. That's another bug. Bird. Bat. Okay, that's a plane. That's a bird with insect wings. That's a plane with feathers. That's an insect. Insect. Bird. Bird. Lots of Birds. John Lithgow. Bird. That's Hitler. Okay, bird. Insect.

S: Thank you for completing these tests.

D: Good Afternoon.

A: Salvon.

D: Now that you've completed your test I'd like to tell you about some the educational programming that we offer on:

S: Salvon!

D: 'The Anthropology of the Santa Claus Experience.' In 1973 Dr. Travis John...

S: Salvon.

D: Conducted a radical experiment which yielded startling results. Using a cross-section of families living throughout New Hampshire, all of which had eleven year-old children, all of which celebrated Christmas, Dr. John...

S: Salvon.

D: Arranged for each family to heap an unusually large amount of Christmas presents upon their eleven year-olds. Dr. John...

S: Salvon.

D: Then arranged for all of the presents to be removed from the house.

A: Needless to say, the majority of these eleven year-old New Hampshire natives were quote unquote 'Heartbroken'.

D: But that was not the end of the experiment. Dr. John...

S: Salvon.

D: Arranged for gifts given to be returned to fifty-percent children after a period of forty-eight hours. The gifts given to the other fifty-percent of the children were destroyed.

A: Dr. John...

S: Salvon.

A: Did follow-up interviews with all of the participating children for the next ten years. Tune in to channel three to find out what he discovered.

S: Are you interested in how stewardesses are trained? Are you interested in the personal life of your stewardess or steward? Would you like to know how you can help a stewardess help herself? Are you interested in becoming a stewardess? If your answer to any of these questions is 'maybe' tune into channel four and find out the answers.

D: All right girls, as always I want you to be polite. Remember that the customer is always right. I want you to remember to smile, and be aware that the customers look to you when there is turbulence. They look to you when they feel sick. They are dependent upon your smiles. Now, as you know, we have begun serving milkshakes. We have chocolate, vanilla, strawberry, soy, and orange. Now, when customers ask for a shake I want you to pause for a moment, look confused, then nod your head as if you understand, stand up straight, and just begin by shaking your hips, then your arms, and eventually I want you to just let your whole body shake, lightly at first, and then very intensely for about fifteen seconds.

A: Additionally, I want you to offer any white members of first-class oral sex for a small fee.

S: But what about my self-respect?

A: If you do it right self-respect should hit the back of your throat after about ten minutes.

S: But I have a boyfriend.

A: That's okay, that's okay, oral sex is not sex, it was invented by fags.

D: That's true, it was invented by fags.

S: But I'm a girl.

A: The more the merrier.

D: It's important that members of first-class understand the difference between them and *coach*.

A: Smiles: wider. Charm: thicker.

D: Rainbow: brighter.

A: Mountains: higher.

D: Pants: tighter.

A: Crash: harder.

D: Drink: harder.

A: Money: harder.

D: Fuck: harder.

A: These are the splendid and heavenly advantages of first-class, this is what we're here for people, this is what stewardesses are for.

D: Protein: bitter.

A: I'd like to remind you that I have all of your teddy bears in the cockpit and I will start tossing them out one by one...

S: Not my teddy bear!!

A: I will toss them out ONE BY ONE – YOURS FIRST – if you girls misbehave. You got me? I am not kidding.

S: Not my teddy-bear. You said you were going to keep them safe. You said you would keep my teddy bear safe.

A: Shut up, you shut your mouth. Your teddy bear is mine. It belongs to me now. You won't get him back unless you please the customers.

S: Not my teddy bear.

A: Now, go and sell those shakes. What am I paying you for?

S: (*To herself.*) You won't kill my teddy bear. My teddy bear can fly. He's stronger than you. I'm stronger than you. My teddy bear can fly and so can I. My teddy bear is worth living for. He's special, he can talk. He's smarter than you. Me and my teddy will win. We always win 'cause we're stronger than all the people who want to hurt us. We'll survive.

D: That's the stewardess information channel. Channel four. Enjoy your flight. Salvon.

A: Members of first-class can tune in to channel ten, where we are offering an interactive workshop covering issues surrounding the defacement of Mercedes Benz automobiles.

D: Are you very rich?

S / A: Salvon.

D: Do you drive a Mercedes Benz?

S / A: Salvon.

D: Has your Mercedes Benz, particularly the triangular hood ornament, been defaced in any way since you purchased the car?

S / A: Salvon.

D: I thought so. Do you people know the statistics on jealousy in this country? They are startling. Truly. We live in a country full of jealous people. Lazy, jealous people. People of such questionable moral status that they actually enjoy owning things which they did not buy with their own money. They enjoy destroying things owned by other people simply because they wish they owned these things themselves. People who burn down their own neighborhoods.

S: Jealous people. Pathetic gossiping people. Lonely, sad little people who, instead of building something of their own, tear down other people. Clingy, black people. Square-jawed fake people. Skinny, ugly people. These are the people who deface the Mercedes Benz.

D: Salvon!

S: These are the people who would rather sleep through darkness than have dreams. These are diseased people. People who wear morality like a new shirt. They use love as a weapon. Their friendships are lonely, paranoid attempts at consolidations of power. Their idea of fun is to wallow in self-pity, occasionally striking out at those they wish to be.

A / D: Salvon!

A: These are the people who deface the Mercedes Benz.

S / D: Salvon!

A: I have no sympathy for these people. They are weak. They are sniveling. They are haters, alcoholics, street scum, frustrated intellectuals, overweight, shoplifting virgins. Rich girls with ghetto accents. Californians!

S / D: Salvon!

A: Californians, with minds and hearts built like hot little suburbs.

S: 'Let's get away from the city. Let's deface a beautiful automobile.' That's my impression of them.

D: 'Oh hello! I'm a car-defacer, aren't I special? I've got a small penis and a drug habit. I like to break other kid's toys.'

A: 'Look at me! I don't have any cake but I'm going to eat cake! How do I do that? Easy, I'll deface a Mercedes Benz!'

D: You get the idea. Americans are desperate to deface your Mercedes Benz. But two can play at this game.

S / A: Salvon.

D: It's very easy. You must treat these defacements as medals of honor. You must welcome, even encourage the vandals. Let them destroy your automobile. Be stronger than them. There is a difference between you and *them.*

S / A: What's the difference?

D: The difference is: You Are Not Defined By Your Belongings. You are a positive, powerful individual, and this would be true no matter what. Embrace the defacement. It is a red badge of courage. Embrace the hostility: It is not everyone that is dynamic enough to be the target of hostility. Consider it one of the many privileges you deserve.

A: Salvon is also offering advanced lectures on issues surrounding Mercedes defacement. Topics for the advanced lectures include:

S: 'Having Sex in Your Mercedes and Not Cleaning Up After Yourself.' This is a dynamic, interactive workshop which covers various ways of documenting your friend's responses when they discover the evidence of sexual play.

D: 'Self-Mutilation: Defacing Your Own Mercedes.' What are the positive ramifications of this practice? What are the psychological results? The Anthropology of the Santa Claus Experience. The Unabomber.

A: 'Mercedes Benz and the Ku Klux Klan.' In 1953 a white Mercedes Benz was the standard Klan-mobile. When did this standard drop? Additional topics covered: Is it possible to enjoy a sexual encounter with someone for whom you have a strong dislike?

S: Salvon, ladies and gentlemen.
Socialization towards pain and privilege.
The doctor is in.

7

Witches:

S: Thirty-thousand feet and climbing.

   Pause.

   Engine failure.

   Pause.

   Salvon?

A: Yes Salvon?

S: Is everybody sleeping?

A: They are sleeping.

   Pause.

S: Salvon?

A: Yes?

S: Are we flying home?

A: Salvon.

S: I'm scared.

D: Don't be scared.

A: Don't be scared.

S: They took my teddy bear from me.

D: He'll survive, he's strong.

S: He's alone without me. He's lonely.

A: He can hear you, feel the beat of your heart.

S: He's crying. I can feel him crying.

D: Tell her a story.

A: Do you want me to tell you a story?

S: I want my teddy.

A: Once upon a time you can't always get what you want. In the land of I'm Not Sure I Understand You. Surrounded by They Put Handcuffs On Flowers.

D: Underneath a huge I've Got To Watch My Back. On the first day of Everyone Is Out To Get Me. On top of the most beautiful Conspiracy To Control And Oppress: There was a girl.

S: That's me.

A: She was the most beautiful child of god. She was surrounded by I Don't Understand Why That's Considered Normal. She was raised by twenty-five I'm Against Everything Normal And Oppressive.

D: And she ate a steady diet of I Was Born Against It All And It Will Always Be That Way. Confused by the similarities between what I am and what I'm against.

A: She was a lonely child...

S: That's me. My teddy bear.

A: Pain made her happy. Fun made her scared, and ashamed.

S: I'm born against. I miss my teddy. I know why I can't cry. It's because sadness makes me happy.

D: Once upon a time I Never Learned How To Rejoice. In the mystical land of People Like To Hurt Other People, Especially Children. Underneath a huge He Taught Me To Be Afraid When He Forced Me To Touch Him. Believing with all her being that The Heart Is Satisfied By Dissatisfaction, and wishing it wasn't true...

A: She went on a journey.

D: She took her teddy.

A: She flew through the sky towards the only thing that makes sense.

D: And when she crashed down she sang...

S: Mountains are inverted valleys.
Fly high.
Crash hard.
My heart will learn to rejoice.

A: And she fell asleep underneath I Can't Make Any Sense Of It. At the hour of Toys Break All The Time. In the year of They Put Handcuffs On Flowers. Beneath the bright, shining, sense of something white, something powerful, something destructive.

   Pause.

D: Do you feel better?

A: Have anything to say for yourself?

   Pause.

S: No.

8

Steve, Stone Sarah:

A: Hello, my name is Salvon and I'll be your Steward today.

D: Steward? What the fuck is this bullshit?

A: Okay. Before I take your order I'd like to inquire as to how you all are feeling today?

S: How am I doing? How do you think I'm doing? I just threw my fucking guts up into a tiny little bag which I thought was my vomit bag but turned out to be my *fucking life-preserver.* My feet fucking *hurt* because I've got all these fucking *corns* which, needless to say, aren't responding well to the altitude.

D: I've got a fucking headache. My fucking seat doesn't go back far enough. These fucking chairs are too small. My fucking food tray is too big. These little plastic cups of water taste like I just cleaned an air conditioner with my tongue and I've got a *fucking erection* which seems to be trying to start a fight with me and I don't know what his problem is but he keeps staring at me and fucking bumping up against me and shit, so *that's* how I'm fucking doing.

A: Okay, my name is Salvon.

S / D: SO WHAT?!!!

A: And I'd like to take your food order.

S: Oh, he'd like to take my food order? Is that what you want to do? Well what are my choices you fucking queer-bait?

A: Chicken or Egg.

D: CHICKEN OR EGG????!!!

S: Can I please, FOR THE LOVE OF JESUS CHRIST, get a fucking VEGETARIAN MEAL on this SHITTY-THIRD-WORLD-CHICKEN-SHACK-AIRPLANE?

A: Uh, yeah, there's no meat in the *egg*.

S: Well, bring it on then!

A: And for the gentleman?

D: I'll TEAR OUT YOUR FUCKING HEART!

A: Okay, be back in a minute.

Pause.

Hey guys, did the food tray come by while I was in the bathroom?

S / D: Yeah.

A: Shit. (*Pause.*) You guys seem mad.

D: Us? No. We're fine. Things are just a little cramped.

A: You should try stretching your legs it really helps with...

D: I'LL TEAR OUT YOUR FUCKING HEART!

S: Do either of you have a tampon?

A / D: (*Both start gagging and retching violently.*) NO, Jesus! (*More retching.*) NO! Absolutely not! Oh... (*More gagging.*) Jesus Sarah do you have to (*They can't breathe.*) say that out loud? (*More coughing and choking.*)

S: I'm serious.

A / D: OH NO! (*They gag and start fake-vomiting.*) That's fucking disgusting! (*More choking and vomiting.*) Sarah, Jesus, please don't, it's... (*Belching.*) ... Jesus save us.

S: What? I just asked for a tampon.

A / D: (*Both retch and vomit more violently than before.*) SARAH! (*Vomiting.*) stop please, it's (*Gagging.*) torture! I'm going to throw up my intestines. (*More heavy breathing and spitting.*)

S: You guys are crazy.

A: Fucking-A Steve could you get your fucking arm off my fucking armrest? Use your LEFT ONE!

D: I'M RIGHT-FUCKING-HANDED.

A: Maybe if you weren't the fucking fattest piece of shit I've ever seen.

D: Maybe if you didn't fidget like a fucking tree monkey, you wouldn't be fucking...

A: Maybe if your mother wasn't the sloppiest whore in Virginia...

D: At least I'm not a fucking gaylord, fucking yuppie-ass...

S: Would you two shut the fuck up I've had it with your fucking bitching and moaning...

A: Oh, shut the fuck up you fucking brainless little fucking tramp...

D: Yeah I've had enough of your fucking mouth and the smell coming off your CUNT...

S: Oh, I'm sorry I doesn't smell like ASS, cause I know that's where you two like to put your DICKS...

A: Do you kiss your kids with that mouth you filthy fucking tramp?

S: No, but you can kiss my ass bitch, you know what time it is!

D: Oh, I know what time it is, I've been fucking hit by a fucking train!

A: That's right you fat train-wreck motherfucker...

S: Yeah, you fucking jelly-belly bitch-ass pussy faggot cocksmoker...

D: Both of you can slurp my fucking tent-pole, all right? You fucking teacher's pet-ass mother-fucking...

S: Shut the fuck up you stupid fucking alcoholic momma's boy...

A: Ugly-ass, open-wound pussy, saggin' titty, skinny little...

D: Bitch-made fucking porch-monkey, squirrel-eatin'...

S: MOTHERFUCKERS!

A: I'll fuck your mother with a fucking baseball bat...

D: I'll fuck you with a twelve-gauge shotgun you cocksucker!

S: I'll scratch your eyes out!

A: JESUS WOULD YOU JUST CALM DOWN!

ALL stand suddenly and salute.

D: Heil Hitler!

S / A: Heil Hitler!

A / S / D: SIEG HEIL, SIEG HEIL, SIEG HEIL, SIEG HEIL!

Pause.

A / S / D: Whew. That's better.

A: It's strange how airplane bathrooms are / always so strange.

S: Always so strange, I know, like a parallel world. / So strange.

D: So strange. Say, have either of you ever played with Legos or put Legos in your mouth?

S: I don't know Steve, the only thing I really put in my mouth is my son's cock.

Long pause.

D: Son's cock? Don't you mean your husband's?

Pause.

S: What did I say?

D: You said your husband's...

A: Cock.

S: Oh, well, you know what I mean. My husband's cock.

A: That's so funny Sarah, and at the same time, so brave of you to say.

S: Thank you. Would you like me to read you this poem my son wrote?

A / D: Sure would.

S: Okay. It's called 'Mommy Loves My'. I know it should be 'Me' but I don't believe in correcting him.

A / D: Okay.

S: *Mommy Loves My*
Mommy loves my so much
she puts me in my chair
and gets all the black elves
to touch me
and touch my teeth
all the time.

Long pause.

A: That's beautiful Sarah, and once again I thought it was brave of you to read it.

D: I agree, not only is your son obviously talented, but you are clearly nothing but an encouraging, supportive figure in his life.

S: It's true, I am. I mean, I know I'm not the only one who hates dumb-looking guys who drink Johnny Walker and talk about the novel they're working on. I know I'm not the only one who thinks you should make eye contact with midgets so that they feel taller on the inside. I'm not the only one who wonders why girls are such embittered back-stabbing little cunts, who seem to be in love with hating each other. I know I'm not alone in this. I know I'm not the only one who thinks so. I know I'm not the only one who thinks that they are, despite all the contrary evidence, inferior. They are. I'm not content. And I'm not alone. I think it's a valid perspective, and it's a perspective which I hope to pass on to my son, no one wants to end up in a room alone with someone like that.

A: Or in a room alone period.

D: I love you guys. I really do.

S: You guys remind me of Hitler.

A: God you are so beautiful.

D: You really are.

S: If Hitler wasn't so crazy, I bet he'd like you guys a lot.

D: People tell me that.

A: MMMMM.

S: You know, the Hitler inside you is hurting, did I ever tell you guys that?

A / D: No.

S: He's on fire. He's hoping someone will learn from him, and use his power for good instead of evil.

9

Airline Staff:

D: Ladies and Gentlemen Salvon. We've reached our cruising altitude and we are well over the Atlantic Ocean. If you look out your window you should be able to see it. Big, and blue, almost like a vast graveya-...oops shut my mouth, bad Salvon, bad Salvon, bad Salvon. Please allow for this entertaining interlude:

A holds a portable electric piano.

A: Hello Ladies and Gentlemen, thanks for flying Salvon. This first song is about situations in life that you can either be smart, and learn from, or ignore and those lessons will pass you by. It's dedicated to everyone out there who feels lost and frustrated sometimes.

He plays for five seconds.

This next song is about a girl I knew who traded in her

personality and became like everyone else because she thought it would make her happy, but it didn't, and that lesson remains unlearned; it's called 'Lesson Unlearned'.

He plays for five seconds.

This song is about brutality and injustice in this country and how it doesn't just hurt minorities and women, but how much it hurts normal people like us just to know about it. It hurts me to see people treated brutally and unjustly, it hurts all of us, it's called 'Tear Down the Wall, ('Cause it's Tearing Me Up)'.

He plays for five seconds.

This song is about how hard it is to express things with words and it's dedicated to a friend of mine who committed suicide and didn't leave a note.

He cries.

S: Good evening ladies and gentlemen. Praise be to Salvon.

A / D: Salvon.

S: Praise be to the Institution of Fear and the Economy of Death.

A / D: Salvon.

S: Praise be to every institution, organization, sub-culture, and social movement.

A / D: Salvon.

S: Praise be to all the child molesters. Praise be to all men with balls enough to take what is rightfully theirs. Praise be to any man who puts his satisfaction in front of someone else's sanity.

A / D: Salvon.

S: He said, 'I've got to get mine. It's all about getting your own and watching your back. Humans are animals. They are cannibals. You need to protect what is yours.' Praise be to him.

A / D: Salvon.

S: Praise be to life-threatening illness and alcoholism. Praise be to messy break-ups and racial injustice, for these are the only torches which illuminate any meaning in this world any more.

A / D: Salvon.

S: Praise be to drowning.

A / D: Salvon.

S: He said: 'I saw this new girl.'

A: 'She looks like a buzzsaw.'

D: 'On Friday nights she makes me want to party in Japan.'

S: 'She's got long brown hair. Green eyes. An olive complexion.'

A: 'She looks like a thirteen year-old boy with breasts.'

D: 'She looks like every Rorschach test I ever took.'

S: 'Every cotton candy lady at every fair.' Now listen very closely because for the next minute I am going to make nothing but sense:

A: Salvon.

D: Salvon.

S: On the trains, midgets converge and plan the overthrow and destruction of the African American population of the United States in hopes of making midgets the new notable minority and…what? Oh I'm sorry: DWARFS! FUCKING DWARFS! FUCKING NATIVE AMERICANS!! Woo woo woo woo woo woo woo woo woo…

A: woo woo woo woo woo woo woo woo woo woo woo woo woo

D: woo woo woo woo woo woo woo woo woo woo woo woo woo

S: The New Notable Minority. The Ku Klux Klan admitted its first black members today! Democrats are calling this a landmark success for Affirmative Action!

A / S / D: woo woo woo woo woo woo woo woo woo woo woo woo

Pause.

S: MIDGETS!

A / S / D: woo woo woo woo woo woo woo woo woo woo woo

A and D begin a 'Native American chant'.

S: Who's scared? Go ahead, testify! Who among us lives in fear? Stand up. I heard you when you walked in here. I can hear everything you say you don't fool me. Come on and stand up and tell us what scares you. Are you scared this plane will crash?

A / D: Salvon.

S: Well it won't! Are you scared that no one will love you??

A / D: Salvon.

S: Well they will! They will until they die! Are you scared that your parents will die while you're away from home?

A / D: Salvon.

S: Well they will.

A: I have something to say, is this all right? Can everyone hear me? I'm going to testify okay? You guys don't know me but I have something to say. I'm not a smart man. I'm not an attractive man. I have fear. I'm not happy all the time. But I believe in progress. I believe that it is possible to make my life better. I can make a commitment right now. A commitment to all of you, and I don't even know you! I'm just meeting you all right now, but I know the difference between right and wrong. I know a lot of things, I went to college, I've had sex before, I've done bad things, *you all know*, we're not perfect. But we can make a promise. We can promise to be better. We can wake up and say 'Hey world, you deserve to see me smile!' 'Hey sun, thank you for shinning today!' 'Hey husband/wife, I love you, I love having sex with you, I like putting it in your mouth.' 'Hey chipmunk, go in peace, make babies.' 'Hey faggots, give me all your money.'

S: Excuse me, I have something to say, is this all right? My name is Susan.

A / D: Hello Susan.

S: And listen, that was beautiful what you just said, and I agree, we can make a change. We don't have to live in fear. We can be powerful and like, organized. For years I was ashamed of myself. I felt really guilty all the time. I had a really tight pussy. I didn't let boys fuck me. Then I met my guru. And he didn't appear in human form, he was a *real* self. And I had sex with him. He put my face in the dirt and I realized I don't need to be ashamed of myself. I'm worth it. My body is mine and YOU can't have it. It's mine, you're not gonna get what I've got, *bitch*, you know what time it is? It's time to get the fuck out of my face unless you wanna get smacked. I've got self respect!

A: I just want to add that these techniques also apply to all you faggots out there 'cause Lord knows you need self-respect more than we do. I mean, seriously, you don't see me on the cover of some magazine telling people my personal business you demented cocksucking dykes.

D: Uh, yes I have something to say. My name is Steve.

A / D: Hello Steve.

D: And I'm really scared that this plane is going to crash. And I think I'm going to cheat on my wife. And I used to wet the bed. And I sometimes I buy books which will make me look smart.

S: That's okay Steve, you can't help it.

A: Life is dangerous.

10

Steve:

S / A: (*Whispering throughout monologue but out of sync with each other.*) You grow up. / No problem. Then something changes. You get scared. Then your heart breaks. You can't help it. Life is dangerous. You grow up. No problem. Then something changes. You get scared. Then your heart breaks.

D: It's not that I'm scared. I'm not scared. I'm not scared. Do I have anything in my teeth? No? Good. Do you have a magazine I could read? Thank you. Do I have anything in my teeth? No? Good. Nice weather we're having. Sure is hot in here. Okay. I think I'm going to cheat on my wife. She won't mind. Okay, I think I heard something. I definitely heard something. Did you hear something? Do I have anything in my teeth? No? Good. Please just keep flying. Just keep flying. Don't crash please. I'll do anything. Okay, Salvon, I'm going to pray. I know I don't normally pray, but I promise I will from now on. Dear Salvon, please deliver me safely. Salvon I rejoice in your heavenly power. You are greater than I. More powerful than I. I can't die. This isn't right. What's going on? Someone tell me what happened? I'm scared. Do I have anything in my teeth? No? Good. This is crazy. I can't die. I'm not made to die. I didn't do anything wrong, could you please stop breathing on me? Thank you. Oh my God did you hear something? I heard something. I definitely heard something. What was that? Oh, Salvon, protect me, save me. Salvon, the oceans boil I know they do. This is crazy. I'm going to cheat on my wife. She won't mind. She doesn't care. I'm not a bad guy. If I was a bad guy she'd care, but I'm not a bad guy. I'm a good guy. Nobody can tell me what to do. You don't know me. You don't know anything about me. You don't care about me, you fucking fakes. I'm a good guy. I pay my taxes. I go down on my wife. I give my kids an allowance. So I don't really think it's fair that I should go down in flames here. It hardly seems fair. Could you please stop breathing on me? What? Do I have something in my teeth? No? Good. Oh I get it. I don't deserve what I've got. You want to take it away from me. Well fuck you you fucking bloodsuckers. If you had what I had you wouldn't be ashamed. You wouldn't feel guilty. Jesus Salvon I don't want to crash, it's not fair, I didn't volunteer for penance. I'm not confessing my sins. I'm not sorry, I don't have any sympathy for you people. LAZY. SCARED. Don't hate me just 'cause you're too scared to live like I do. It's survival of the fittest you fucking jew cunt. It's natural selection. That's why the monkeys still swing from the trees. That's why there's blood on the fields you fucking cunts. What? Do I have something in my teeth? Well maybe I'll put my fist through yours. I'm a good guy. I AM VERY SENSITIVE and I am going to pour the last pint of blood down your throat. I'm not confessing any sins. I am not scared. I said: I am not scared of you. The last word is I'll see you in hell right after I *fuck* your daughter in the backyard of your fucking dirty ghetto housing project you fucking degenerate. CHEAT ON MY WIFE. She won't care. If I was a bad guy she'd care but I'm not a bad guy.

Pause. D picks up the whisper chant.

S: (*Calmly.*) This one goes out to all my new-age motherfuckers. All my plane-crash niggas. All my corporate blood-brain niggas. All my nigga niggas, cut into a thousand pieces, cast your ashes into the ocean. To all my wigga niggas. To all my white-trash Jerry Springa niggas. This one goes out to all my new-age motherfuckers. All my plane-crash niggas. All my corporate blood-brain niggas. All my nigga niggas, cut into a thousand pieces, cast your ashes into the ocean, to all my wigga niggas, to my white-trash Jerry Springa niggas.

11

Steve, Stone and Sarah:

D: I heard we'll be flying with a convention of child molesters today.

S: Also: the Shriners.

A: I also heard about the child molesters. Are they going to Spain?

S: They're not. They're getting off in New Hampshire.

A: Did you ever read that book *Getting Off In New Hampshire*?

S: Actually I did, but I have to say I didn't really / care about the characters.

A: Care about the characters? I mean, if I don't care about the characters, I have no personal or emotional investment in the story.

S: I know Jesus would say it's important to care about every character, even if they are reprehensible, but I just don't think the teachings of Jesus are relevant in this day and age.

D: *Getting Off in New Hampshire.*

S: Don't get me wrong. I love Jesus Christ. I'm not one of those Halloween Hunters, my father was a fisherman, I just don't think that at such a critical moment in history we have room enough to pile our trash against the walls.

D: I couldn't agree with you more. Especially with your use of the word 'trash'.

A: I'm a sentimental guy; I cry in front of the mirror. But if I don't care about the characters? Watch out. I'm very intolerant, especially when it comes to my entertainment. For example: Las Vegas is somewhat misleading.

S: I'm serious about my opinions. Jesus does play a role in my life, but then again, you never know, my world-view could easily change based on what I'm about to read in this magazine.

A: What are you about to read?

S: I don't know! Anything! Articles about whales, someone selling baby food, a personals ad I'm not eligible for. My rules are not set in stone.

Lights out.

D: Salvon, night has fallen.

The sound of engine failure.

12

Airline Staff:

D: Ladies and gentlemen there has been a hydraulic failure. I know many of you are scared. Now is the time to put your faith in Salvon. I want you to direct your attention to your video monitors. We will now present you with Emergency Entertainment: The Safety Mantras. Repeat after each phrase Salvon. Salvon can help. BEGIN EMERGENCY ENTERTAINMENT:

D: Good Afternoon.

S / A: Salvon.

D: This is your captain speaking.

S: And I would like to review the safety measures with you.

D: We have just one rule:

S / A: Salvon.

D: The Heart Is Not Satisfied By Dissatisfaction.

S: Good afternoon Salvon, how is the chicken?

A: Let me explain:

D: The pursuit of safety is not in and of itself satisfactory. One can succeed or fail, and these are the means by which we measure our satisfaction.

S / A: Salvon.

S: But the pursuit of safety is not satisfying.

A: And the Heart Is Not Satisfied By Dissatisfaction.

D: There must, therefore, be a realization of safety.

S / A: Salvon.

D: I am not suggesting an abstraction. I am suggesting a *rebirth.*

S: Please buckle your seat belts.

D: You must be reborn into a transformed state, a state beyond self. A state of realized safety which embraces both the crash and the landing simultaneously. A state which is brought on by the recognition of me, transformed by the *communion* with me.

A: Realized Static Safety.

S: Satisfaction.

S / D / A: SALVON.

A: Hello, its me.

S / D: Salvon.

A: And I forgot what I'm supposed to believe in today. Could you please remind me?

S: Okay, you believe in milk.

D: Photography.

S: And dashboard dials.

D: You believe that capitalism is wrong.

S: And that black people are just like us.

D: Except when they're different.

S / A: Salvon.

A: Except when they're midgets.

S / D: Salvon.

A: Hello there!

S / D: Salvon!

A: How are you doing?

D: Fine.

A: How was your summer?

D: Great.

A: How's your mother? I have to go to her house tonight and get my cock. I left it inside her vagina.

D: My mother is fine.

A: How's your father. I heard there has been an increase in wiggers this year.

D: My father is good.

S / A: Salvon.

D: And yes, I've noticed a marked increase in the wigger population.

A: Oh good –

S / D: Salvon.

A: – I'm not the only one.

S: Hello people it's me!

A / D: Salvon.

S: And today we will learn how to have a conversation.

A: Begin with a word like 'hello', 'excuse me', or 'hey'.

D: Follow it with a proper noun.

S: Then just follow your instincts! I'm sure they'll be correct! Just don't ask them their weight, age, or income.

D: Ask them what they do or what they *like*.

A: And if they are stand-offish, unresponsive, or if it just seems like you're not getting anywhere:

A / D: THAT'S A CONVERSATION!

S / A: SALVON!

S: Nothing is accomplished unless you manage to get your cock inside them.

D: Or get them to… (*He swallows.*)

A: Put something in your vagina.

S: Guys, you can ignore that one.

D: Remember:

A: Salvon.

S: Loneliness Is Not A Sin.

D: But something else is.

A: So be careful.

D: Good evening.

S / A: Salvon.

D: In 1981 someone said: 'I am very skeptical of all this love stuff. If love is meaningful and true, why don't we feel good all the time?'

A: To which another person replied: 'Some people haven't found love.'

S: And another person said: 'Love is just a word, a general term which, if anything, limits our ability to feel truly and freely.'

D: A fourth person replied: 'Hey faggots, give me all your money.'

S: And they did. Which proves that love doesn't exist, so fuck it.

D: You're only as big as the scars on your arms, bitch.

A: My idea of closure with you involves gasoline and a match.

S: Salvon.

S: Good Evening!

A / D: Salvon.

S: I'd like to speak to just the anorexics in the audience.

A: Whether you know it or not girls, you're on the right track. But there is a problem.

D: I'm bulimic and I have something to say: 'Girls, you've been misled.'

S: That's right girls, 'You've been misled'. Anorexia is the eating disorder of the past. It's empty, unsatisfying, and very, very boring.

A: Bulimia, on the other hand, is enriching, effective, and fun!

S: Salvon.

A: Imagine, the pleasure of eating and the pleasure of throwing up. Everyone likes to throw up! You always feel better afterward! So why not try it?

S: We live in a society devoid of ritual. Be the first girl on your block to have one. Be the first girl on your block who doesn't look like a fat bloated pig and boys will put their penises in your vagina.

A / D: Salvon.

D: Dear Salvon.

A: How are you?

S: I'm fine.

A: Salvon?

S: Yes sister?

A: Girls are mysterious creatures.

S: Yes they are. What are they?

A: Girls are mysterious creatures.

S: Salvon.

A: Ear Hungry.

S: Quiet.

A: Eternal.

D: Salvon:

A: Wrestles with doubt.

D: Salvon:

A: Has the crowd on his side.

S / D: Salvon:

A: Resembles the architecture that surrounds her.

S: Salvon.

A: 'I loved a girl once.'

D: 'A long time ago.'

S: Salvon.

A: Fuck this fucking memory.

D: (*Screaming.*) LUCKY FOR US WE LIVE ON THE FIRST FLOOR!

A: Salvon.

S: Can I ask you a few questions?

D: Yes you can, you sure can.

S: What is your name?

A / D: Salvon.

S: Where were you born?

A / D: Salvon.

S: Are you satisfied?

D: Am I satisfied at thirty-thousand feet? I am that which is at one with the earth. I am a brain-sized spaceman. I am joy, the resurrection. I am culture-sized, earth-sized.

S: Do you ever wake up in the morning and wonder how you find things to talk about every day?

D: Never. I am interested in a wide range of topics. I like all kinds of music except for country and rap. I enjoy discussing politics and sex. I like talking about people I know or places I've been. I like winking and signaling. I like buying things for people and reminiscing about the Good Old Days. I like going to the bathroom and wandering from place to place.

S: I like creeping into my baby's room late at night and smelling the back of his neck. I like watching him breathe and knowing that I created him and he will always love me as long as I give him money. I love my baby. I enjoy buying him cute expensive clothes and cleaning his waste. I like screwing my husband and counting the number of times he closes his eyes and thinks about other women.

A: I LIKE GOING TO THE MALL!

D: LUCKY FOR US WE LIVE ON THE FIRST FLOOR!

A: I LIKE GOING TO THE MALL! I like going to the beach. I like going to parties. I like throwing parties. I like to attend parties. I like going to work. I like coming home from work. I like traveling and standing still. I like alcohol. YEAH! I like alcohol and all the pain it takes away. I like going to funerals and weddings. I like bar mitzvahs. Hell, I like BAT mitzvahs. I like going for quiet walks in the park. And maybe, if I'm feeling randy, I'll rape a couple of sixteen year-old girls. And maybe, if I'm feeling randy, I'll report the rapes to the police and mention that a black guy did it. And maybe if I'm feeling randy I'll go and watch the execution. I watched them execute John Hinckley Jr. Boy, did it make me hard!

D: I like thinking about things and understanding things. I like playing GUITAR! I like screwing my wife and imagining she is a supermodel, or a porn star, or my daughter, or my sister, or my mother. I like being WHITE, let's just get it all out in the open OKAY?

S / D / A: AS LONG AS WE'RE GOING TO CRASH!

S: Let's be honest! Honesty is the best policy! I like being white. I like picket fences. I like Hitler. I don't agree with what he said but at least he said something! Right?

I like being nice to midgets. Midgets are so poor and unfortunate. Someone has to be nice to them. Someone has to go out of their way to make them feel tall on the inside. Why not me? I've got the time. I've got a lot of spare time. I SURE DO HAVE A LOT OF SPARE TIME WHEN I'M NOT GOING TO PTA MEETINGS, when I'm not polishing my silver, when I'm not making midgets feel taller on the inside! They deserve it, it's not their fault they're black! I mean, COME ON:

S / D / A: WE'RE LUCKY WE LIVE ON THE FIRST FLOOR!

D: And in conclusion I'd like to say that honesty is the best policy.

A: I'd like to conclude with a question: Are we really going to crash right now? / I DON'T UNDERSTAND.

S: I don't understand! People like me don't get pregnant Barbara! I would never hurt something, especially something that came from me!

A: I don't understand, are we going to crash right now?

S: Please don't tell me we're going to crash right now!

A: I can't shake this feeling of absolute fury.

S: I'll shatter every bone in my left hand against the back of your soft skull you pathetic skinny little cunt!

A: Don't make me mad or I'll write a play about it!

S: Are we really going to crash right now?

A: I don't want to crash.

S: Where is the best place to sit on the plane?

A: What do we do if crash at sea?

S: Are we really going to crash right now?

A: DON'T TELL ME, I DIDN'T EVEN GET TO FIND OUT WHAT HAPPENED TO ALL THOSE KIDS WHOSE CHRISTMAS PRESENTS WERE DESTROYED BY DR. TRAVIS JOHN!

D: Salvon!

S: Well, what happened? What's going to happen?

Silence.

D: (*Intercom voice.*) There has been a complete hydraulic failure.
We are currently drifting towards the ocean.
I can't imagine there being any survivors.
This concludes our Emergency Entertainment.
You're on your own.
In conclusion I'd like to say that honesty is the best policy.
And if all of you hadn't been so afraid of crashing, we might not have.
Thank you ladies and gentlemen.
Salvon.
Salvon.
1988.

13

Steve, Stone and Sarah:

The following is apocalyptic, frantic, awful.

A: WELL THAT'S JUST GREAT!

S: I'm tired of it.

D: Hello, out there, can I get a fucking wet nap?

S: I know, why don't you start from the back?

A: Open wide your tonsils give me an erection.

D: Get me a fucking parachute or I'll split you like a fat kid's pumpkin.

A: I won't just pop your cherry, I'll drop a fucking Napalm on that shit....

A / D: FROM THE TOP ROPE!

S: WHERE IS MY TEDDY BEAR?

D: I'm going to cheat on my wife.

S: No don't Steve.

D: I'm going to cheat on my wife. What's the fucking difference?

S: Don't cheat on your wife.

D: We're dead. What's the difference. My rules aren't set in stone.

A: Especially at thirty-thousand feet.

S: Don't cheat on your wife.

D: She won't know the difference.

S: She'll know the difference. I know. My children already know I'm dead.

D: I'm going to cheat on my wife.

A / S: Don't do it.

A: Or do it, I don't care.

D: I've fucked her a hundred times.

A: Secrets never hurt anyone.

S: Curiosity killed the cat.

D: She killed the cat. I haven't fucked her in months.

S: Why now? Why cheat now?

D: I'm tired of it. That's all. Okay? Every night in the same bed. Every night the same words. Over and over. I swore I'd never be like that. I've got to feel like a man. I've got to chop down trees. When I tell my jokes I want the audience to laugh. I want the tigers to cooperate in their cages. Say 'Salvon'.

S / A: Salvon.

D: Stone knows what I mean.

A: I don't know what you mean.

D: You know what I mean Sarah. You do. I want to cheat on my wife. She won't know the difference. She doesn't even know we're married. We haven't fought in years. Let me ask you a question:

S / A: Salvon.

D: What if second chances were like pennies?

S: Would you throw them away?

A: Save them to cash in for something better?

D: Or would they sit in that jar that says: 'Take one if you need it, leave on if you don't'?

S / A: Salvon.

D: I've seen the spot she stares at on the ceiling. I've seen it. It's like she burned it with her eyes. Can't tell me, I read her like a menu. I've seen the discoloration on the wall, discolored by her fucking boredom brown eyes.

S: Maybe she stares at it because it's discolored.

D: Chicken or the egg! CHICKEN OR THE EGG! I'm lonely. YOU HEAR ME? I'm lonely.

A: Lucky for us we live on the first floor.

S: Affairs of the heart are a cruel son of a bitch.

A / D: Salvon.

D: (*Intercom voice.*) Ladies and Gentlemen. This is your captain. You've got about ten minutes.

S / A: Jesus Christ.

A: Sarah?

S: Yes?

A: You think I could put my penis in your vagina?

S: Yes.

A: Yes?

S: Sure. When we crash down.

A: You mean the plane?

S: Probably.

A: Did you mean me?

S: Possibly.

A: My father?

S: No.

A: Oh.

S: Breakfast cereal.

A: I'm into that.

S: Open-minded.

A: People always tell me I'm open-minded.

S: Me too.

A: What about Steve?

S: He's sleeping.

A: Yeah, night is falling.

S: You're cute.

A: I try.

S: Try harder, you're making me drool.

A: Well, I've got more napkins where that came from.

S: Don't flirt with me.

A: Why?

S: I'm like most girls: incredibly fragile.

A: I'm like most boys: already broken.

S: I don't think you're smart.

A: That's fine.

S: I'm just trying to get back at the world.

A: This is as good a place as any.

S: I'm saving all my vomit in jam jars.

A: I'd like to see your collection.

S: I've got it arranged by color.

A: So does everyone.

S: I've decided I'm not going to fuck.

A: Why not? Why fucking not? (*He grabs her around the throat.*) You just came on to me you cheap fucking cunt. Fucking lousy tease cunt. Fucking bitch. Don't you fucking tease me you fucking cunt.

S: I didn't come on to you Stone.

A: The fuck you didn't. Sounded like your plan.

S: I'd like to hear what you hear sometime Stone? I'd like to tune in to that frequency. I'm sure it's a treat. Like broadcasts from the mirror. A frequency so high it can only be heard by dogs.

A: Fuck you trick.

S: You're pathetic. You're weak. I know your type. The worst kind of wallflower.

D: Why don't you shut the fuck up?

S: Fuck you.

D: Fuck me? I wonder who thought that one up? Your mom and dad? Did your pervert uncle teach you that one you fucking cunt? You disgust me.

S: You don't hear a word. You're like an animal.

D: Who wrote it for you? Who wrote it for you?

S: Fuck you Steve.

D: Who wrote the book of love?

A: Salvon.

D: Chapter one:

S: No.

D: CHAPTER ONE: I'm in love and I can't stand to be fucked!

S: Shut your mouth.

D: CHAPTER TWO: I'd rather dance in a room than do anything else. I'm a priss.

S: (*Screaming.*) SHUT YOUR MOUTH!

D: I'm a predetermined priss. A tease. Teasing my fucking tease. God is love love is God and I'm rooting for the chicken! I've been laid out and I know just what to do. I'll get married. I'll live on level eight with my cats and my elegant cock and I'll drink wine till I bust a fucking gut. CHAPTER THREE: Fuck me I need a good fuck.

S: You don't know anything about me. You're a boy. A pathetic little boy. The worst kind of wallflower. You tell me I'm predetermined, you're more slave than man. You think because you're lonely that makes you wise? You think 'cause you're lonely that makes you the elder statesman? It makes you a lonely man and that's all it makes you. My life isn't a fucking photograph Steve. My life isn't a joke.

D: But it's funny to me Sarah. It really is. It's a fucking rib cracker. Flip the page, flip the page. What have we here? A gob of fancy talk? How impressive. CHAPTER FOUR: You adapt to your surroundings better than sand on a beach you fucking cunt. You're a fake. It all makes perfect sense to you doesn't it? Well I'm not fooled.

A: I've been here before, I've been here before, I've been here before. This isn't new to me. I've worn these clothes before. I used to walk differently. I broadcast from a different station. I had a different boss. Then I wanted a change.

S / D: Salvon.

A: I tried to play a different tune, but they saw it on my face. Dogs can smell fear. Keep your hands balled into fists and they won't get at your fingers. Hear it in the tone of my voice. Read my eye movement. I'm a fake.

S / D: Salvon.

A: I'm afraid this is camp to me. No one knows me. But I don't risk anything. My wife is dead. They say I should move on with my life. What the hell does that mean? What the fuck does that mean?

S: Salvon.

A: I scream at myself over and over: 'Don't be weak. Don't be weak. Don't be weak.' But it's no use. I'm weak. If I was fat I'd become a fag. I've noticed fat fags still get laid.

S: That's beautiful. You're really a genius.

A: What are you? Ashamed? My first daughter's name is ashamed. Her boyfriend tells me she grew up to be a pretty hot fuck.

S: You make me sick to my stomach. You're a virus.

A: And you're still as ashamed as I am. Everyone is. Everyone is as ashamed as I am. Look at what we did. Look around. A writhing mass of sniveling, self-centered, brain-dead alcoholics. Worms. Fucking maggots whose idea of having dreams is reading books about fictional characters who have dreams. We're cut off from everything God calls good: Strength, happiness, love, hope: Synonyms for shit. That which has gone the way of the dinosaur. Shit excrement. We belong in the gas chambers. Raped, robbed, and mutilated, singing slave hymns and watching television. That's what we are! That's what we should look like.

S: You have no faith, no faith in anything. You're so self-centered. You're so self-centered you actually think your problems have no end, they just keep going and going to the end of the universe, and suddenly your pathetic pain is an epidemic, your cold sore is the plague, your paranoia is God's disease.

A: When's the last time you really hurt?

S: When's the last time you had anything to compare it to?

D: Lucky for me I live on the first floor bullshit. I don't even have the guts to be a good recluse. I don't have the guts to cheat. I don't have the guts to die.

S: We're going to die.

A / D: Salvon.

S: I'm not scared. Night is falling.

A: I know, I can see it.

S: What did he say?

D: We are drifting slowly towards the ocean.

S: Tell me a story.

A: There aren't any stories.

S: Please.

A: Once upon a time you can't always get what you want.

D: In the land of I'm Not sure I Understand You.

S: I want my teddy.

A: Salvon.

S: I'm sorry for what I am. I try to be different. I am different. Tell me a story.

D: Once upon a time I Never Learned How To Rejoice. In the mystical land of People Like To Hurt Other People. Pain made her happy. Fun made her scared.

S: I miss my teddy. I can hear him crying.

A and D whisper the following continuously but out of sync, like a final prayer, as S speaks.

A / D: Once upon a time you can't always get what you want. In the land of I Don't Understand You. In the year of They Put Handcuffs On Flowers. At the hour of Toys Break All The Time. Underneath a bright, shining I Never Learned To Rejoice. In the land of I Don't Understand You. In the year of They Put Handcuffs On Flowers. At the hour of Toys Break All The Time. Underneath a bright, shining I Never Learned To Rejoice. In the land of I Don't Understand You......

S: People ask me:
 'What's wrong with you?'
 'What's wrong with you?'
 'Are you okay?'
 'Are.'
 'You.'
 'Okay.'
 'What's wrong?'
 I say: 'What's wrong is that nothing is.'
 I'm unhappy because there is nothing to cry about.
 I'm sad because I'm blessed.
 And I don't deserve it.
 I don't know what to do with it.
 It's balsa wood to me.
 I break everything.
 I'm spoiled rotten.
 Sick of being healthy.
 'Are you okay?'

A and D are echoing some of her words.

 I can't convince you that I am.
 I have no past to draw upon.
 No friends whose voices are like lullabies.
 My telephone is dusty.
 I'm obsessed with rock.
 I'm alone, surrounded by every person stupid enough to
 love me.
 My sickness is shame.
 Spoiled Rotten.
 Spoiled Rotten.
 SPOILED ROTTEN.
 SPOILED ROTTEN.

D: SPOILED ROTTEN.

A: ARE YOU OKAY?

S: I'm numb. There is no through line.

A: No connective tissue.

Just a child's collage,
of the good and the bad,
the eventful and the boring,
held together by numbness,
and lies.
I do what my friends do.

D: I do what my friends do.

S: Crash down.

A: I think about suicide.
I'm not smart enough.
To enjoy what I have.
I'm complicated.
Weak.
Morbidly insecure.

D: 'ARE YOU OKAY? WHAT'S WRONG WITH YOU?
WHAT'S WRONG WITH YOU?'

A: What's wrong with me is that I'm alive

S: in a world of beauty,

D: filled with love,

S: flowers,

D: and caring,

A: and I spend every waking moment looking for a mirror,

S: so I can look into it,

A: and remind myself that I'm ugly.

D: I'm starved for pain and depression.

S: I'm desperate to crash.

A: I'm desperate to crash.

D: Deliver me from this hurricane.

S: Lead me to the light.

A: Lay me down in green grass fields.

D: Kiss my forehead.

A: Pour water on my neck.

S: Make a circle of dirt on my stomach.

D: And lower me into the ground.

> *Plane crashes. Deafening noise. Set is destroyed. Noise subsides.*
> *Diminishing drones. Darkness.*

S: Where is my teddy?
I can't see it through the fog.
I can't see it.
Is it torn apart?
Is it torn apart?
I can't see it.
My teddy can fly.
I can fly.
Salvon?

D: Yes sister.

S: Do we fly home tomorrow?

D: Yes sister.

S: I'm scared.

D: Salvon.

S: Tell me a story.

D: Salvon.

End

VICTORY AT THE DIRT PALACE

Characters

K MANN

JAMES MANN

SPENCE

ANDREW

Notes on production

In *Victory at the Dirt Palace* most of the action takes place in two television news studios Much of the dialogue takes place on speaker-phones, cell phones and intercom. James Mann and K Mann are father and daughter. They are employed by competing networks as prime time news broadcasters.

Victory at the Dirt Palace, a Riot Group production, was first performed at La Val's Subterranean Theater, Berkeley California, on July 22, 2002, and subsequently opened at the Edinburgh Fringe Festival on August 4, 2002 at the Garage Theatre. In January 2003, *Victory at the Dirt Palace* opened at Riverside Studios, London. The cast was as follows:

K MANN,   Stephanie   Viola

JAMES MANN,   Paul Schnabel

SPENCE,   Adriano Shaplin

ANDREW,   Andrew Friedman

Directed and designed by The Riot Group

Sound by Adriano Shaplin

Stage Managed by Maria Shaplin

In August 2002 *Victory at the Dirt Palace* received the Scotsman Fringe First Award and the Herald Angel Award. The Riot Group were nominated for a Stage Award for Best Ensemble.

VICTORY AT THE DIRT PALACE

1

JAMES MANN's office. JAMES is seated. K MANN, his daughter, is combing his hair. ANDREW, JAMES' assistant, keeps in touch through an intercom. SPENCE, K's assistant, is on speakerphone.

JAMES: Do I live in a world of Salvon?
A world of serious nonsense and half-hearted tragedy?
An upside-down castle where yes is no and sex is painful?
Or is my world simple to name?
Give it six letters moving left to right and it will be ordered and neat.
Surrounded by lies, we twist in the wind.
Stop my teeth from chattering.

K: Sit still.

JAMES: I am a neutral fool, and the image I create is false as teeth, white and straight.
Teeth, when hungry they tear,
when vicious they bite,
when aroused they click and break against the gates of another.
That my teeth are fake, white and straight, precludes all abandon.
Even my most passionate hunger is executed with hollow precision
and sterile agility.
Thank my bloodless teeth.

SPENCE: I'll have her in the car by six-forty-five. Stand by.

JAMES: Fill me with your sour puss
Until I am milk-fed, fat as a baby
Replace my words with moans
and drown my brain in sex.

SPENCE: K, we've got five minutes.

K: Fine.

ANDREW: Thirty minutes Jim.

JAMES: Salvon.

K: You've got a half hour call?

JAMES: My preference.

SPENCE: I'm moving the car up to the south exit K.

K: I'm going to use my five minutes.

SPENCE: Fine, five minutes.

K: Run the Washington piece by me.

ANDREW: Jim?

JAMES: Not tonight. I'm a big flap-jack.

ANDREW: I'm obliged to ask.

JAMES: Terrible thing these obligations.

ANDREW: Your mouth is moving but I can't hear the...wait...you have dentures.

JAMES: I say: terrible things these obligations. Life is Eden but for the things required of us.

K: I'd rather choke on sloth, raw.

SPENCE: Yeah you would.

JAMES: That's a report I wouldn't mind making. 'Man drowns between sofa cushion.'

K: 'Television looks on helplessly.'

JAMES: 'He was never a strong swimmer.'

ANDREW: Twenty-five minutes Jim.

JAMES: Hey kid, did you find your purse?

K: My wallet? No. Spence?

SPENCE: Yes?

K: Call AmEx and cancel my cards.

SPENCE: I'm doing it.

JAMES: You can't fool me kid.

K: Right. Want to get hammered?

JAMES: Yes!

SPENCE: K, the car is out front, we're going to need to push off...

K: Fuck it, Spence. I don't need to sit through the goddam lighting check.

JAMES: Who know the depths to which dogs will sink?

K: Not me. Do the Washington piece.

JAMES: Oh right: 'We live in uncertain times. What was once a land of forthright honesty and bare knuckle economic growth has become a house of cards where double dealing, backroom bargains, and secretive transactions are the norm. But tonight we're going to shed some light on the...'

K: Stop tilting your head 'knowingly'.

JAMES: That's my subliminal trademark.

SPENCE: AmEx is on the phone. Tell me your account number.

JAMES: 'But tonight we're going to shed some light on the invisible world of political corruption and corporate greed. Our man in Washington' blah blah.

K: Hold on. 4832 281 54 886. Try it in your own words.

JAMES: What?

SPENCE: The number.

K: Spence?

SPENCE: What?

K: Ask them the most recent purchases made.

SPENCE: Okay.

K: Try it in your own words.

JAMES: My own words? 'We live in uncertain times. I work for Jews. Hebrews polished to look like silver dollars and still I hunt for truth.'

SPENCE: Whoa.

K: What?

SPENCE: They bought a six-hundred dollar piece of chocolate.

JAMES: Tonight, grasp tightly the arms of your throne and hear this tale of corruption and greed. Buried in soot...

K: What else?

JAMES: ...we crawl desperately toward light.

SPENCE: Lots of books actually.

K: Titles?

JAMES: Allow me to be your shepherd; handshakes and invisible ink.

SPENCE: *The Terrible Reality of Closet Space.*

JAMES: Every back comes with a knife and no shortage of hands to stab.

SPENCE: *The Racy World of Scentless Metal.*

JAMES: Are we getting hammered or not?

SPENCE: *The Broken Legs of American Tyranny.*

K: Are these self-help books?

JAMES: You know babe, that haircut looks terrible.

K: What?

SPENCE: *The Absolute Mathematics of Sexual Dysfunction.*

JAMES: You look like a goddam kitten.

SPENCE: *Kiss the Kind Face of Kittens.*

K: I look sophisticated.

ANDREW: I saw it, it looks terrible.

JAMES: Mother says you eat ice cream three meals a day.

K: Fine. That's wonderful. I'm leaving. Spence, bring the car around.

SPENCE: These are self-help books.

K: Bring the car around!

SPENCE: I'm right downstairs, do you want me to come up?

K: No. Best of luck tonight Dad, I mean it.

K kisses his cheek goodbye. SPENCE wheels K to her broadcast desk. ANDREW wheels JAMES to his broadcast desk.

JAMES: Lying Tart.

K: I'm coming down Spence, don't cancel that card.

SPENCE: Why?

JAMES: I need to talk to you later kid.

K: About?

JAMES: Be careful with the assistants K, your mother was my copy editor at CCB.

K: Call me.

JAMES: Salvon.

K: Salvon.

2

K is now in her own office.

SPENCE: You're doing an interview with CNC.

K: When?

SPENCE: Thirty seconds. Look straight ahead.

K: What's the research?

SPENCE: It's a short teaser for the local affiliates. Travis John is doing the interview, and it'll run on four-hundred local news programs as the last news item before sports.

K: Before sports?

SPENCE: K, we're not going to get four-hundred affiliates to ditch their closer...fifteen seconds.

K: Kiss a dirty kitten!

SPENCE: Be nice. What's wrong with your hair?

K: I'm going to punch your face. There will be no hugs and kisses.

SPENCE: Five seconds, four, three, two, one...

K: Just punches in your face.

TRAVIS JOHN (SPENCE): Hello. Ms. Mann, thank you for being with us.

K: It's a privilege Travis, thanks for talking to me.

TRAVIS JOHN: You're a controversial figure in the high stakes game of network news. Many people questioned your decision to use the Mann name, given your father's reputation. You're known for being extremely private, even by current standards, and your approach to television journalism, particularly your purist approach to 'hard news', has raised more than a few eyebrows. Now, my question to you is: What is your favorite food?

K: That's a good question, Travis.
I'm glad you're giving me the chance to address this issue.
My favorite thing to eat is octopus.
Raw octopus.
When there is no raw octopus:
I'll take pork. With mashed yams.
No pork?
Fried Chicken and Vodka.
In the absence of all these things I'll eat deviled eggs and honey-friend bacon.

TRAVIS JOHN: Remarkable. Tonight your Evening News broadcast moves from 6:30 to 7:00pm, putting you in direct competition with your father's program. 'World News Tonight with James Mann' has been on the air for thirty years: Nervous?

K: There is nothing to eating animals, Travis.
Someone else brains them, guts them, washes them, grinds them.
I just chew.

TRAVIS JOHN: Remarkable. Thank you for speaking with us K.

K: My pleasure.

SPENCE: Clear.

K: Color me bad!

Dialogue and action now occurs simultaneously in both offices.

JAMES: Show me this morning's copy.

K: Give me the copy Spence.

ANDREW: Are you sure that would be productive?

K / JAMES: Productive?

SPENCE: Let me just read it out loud.

JAMES: Am *I* doing an interview?

ANDREW: *New York Times*: 'Mann to Mann: The Nightly News Wars Heat Up.'

K: Christ. 'Mann to Mann.'

JAMES: 'Mann to Mann.' Bet that burns her ass.

SPENCE: *Chicago Sun Times*: 'The Trusted Crank and his...'

K: What?

ANDREW: I don't really know what this means.

JAMES: I didn't hear you.

SPENCE: 'The Trusted Crank and his Icy Daughter.'

K: Icy?

JAMES: Trusted?

ANDREW: Could mean anything really. They might be comparing your warmth to her...direct style.

JAMES: You don't have to mince words with me, my daughter's a cold bitch. Next.

SPENCE: *The National Review*: 'The So-Called Mann War: Only problem is trying to figure out which one is more liberal.'

JAMES: Her.

K: Him.

ANDREW: *The Nation*: 'Only problem is trying to figure out which one is more conservative.'

JAMES: Bully for them.

SPENCE: *The Village Voice*: 'Only problem is trying to figure out which one is more *dull.*'

K: All right, take them off my goddam source list.

ANDREW: Your idea.

JAMES: Fine keep going.

SPENCE: *The Gay Times*: 'Only problem is trying to figure out which one is more queer.'

K: Son of a bitch!

JAMES: COLOR ME BAD!

ANDREW: Well, I'm surprised it's a point of contention really.

JAMES: What does that imply about me?

K: I'm not butch AT ALL.

SPENCE: Not butch. Queer. Like Queer-bait. I think they're suggesting that Jim is a little...

JAMES: Fey. They think I'm Fey.

K: I'm being type-cast as some kind of foxy tart with daddy issues.

ANDREW: Does 'fey' mean 'gay'?

K: If I'm so butch why do I even bother with this alligator shit make-up?

SPENCE: *Herald Tribune*: 'Trash News, Dodgy Codgers, and Feminist Bobcats: The Rise and Fall of the New TV Royalty.'

K / JAMES: The 'Fall'?

JAMES: What goddam 'fall'?

K: The royalty part is nice though. I'm going to use that.

K pulls out a pair of hand-weights and starts to lift.

JAMES: Get her on the phone.

ANDREW: 864475. What if Spence answers?

JAMES: Don't be afraid of Spence boy.

K: How long do I have?

SPENCE: Fifteen minutes. Hold on. Hello?

ANDREW: Um…hi. I need to speak with K… I need to…

SPENCE: How did you get this job?

ANDREW: Spence, put her on, I've got James here.

SPENCE: Who is it who calls me? Who is it that utters my familiar name and beckons me to famous toil and empty performance?

ANDREW: Can we skip this?

SPENCE: Not a chance stutter freak. Hit me up. Come on! Who is it who calls me?

ANDREW: 'Tis I prince and though your butter soft song tickles my short hairs I must request the attention of His Majesty's famous daughter.

SPENCE: (*To K.*) It's Jim.

K: Put him on speaker.

SPENCE: (*To ANDREW.*) Call me later flap jack.

ANDREW: Kiss a dirty kitten.

SPENCE: Shut your mouth dirty dirty!

K: Put him on speaker! What is it Dad, are you reading the clippings?

JAMES: Kid, I don't read the clippings, we're newsreaders not celebrities, that's a lesson you still need to learn.

K: I'm counting to three.

JAMES: Don't you dare pull that shit with me...

K: One!

JAMES: Okay Okay Okay, I'm fine I'm fine. Don't count to three.

K: What do you want dad? I'm picking out underwear for the broadcast.

K is still lifting the weights.

JAMES: Listen, I'm serious now, I think you got a bum shake on that super-cut.

K: What?

JAMES: Do something about the hair, kid. It's not you.

K: Shut up dad. Hold on. Check back with the credit card company... I want to hear what else they bought.

SPENCE: The people who stole your purse?

K: My wallet. Dad? Listen to me for a second.

JAMES: What is it.

K: I think you should take a drink of water and catch your breath.
Crack your knuckles.
Do a vocal warm up.
Eat a candy bar.
Okay?
Do you want a drink?

JAMES: I want minor plastic surgery.

K: Great. Whatever helps. But we need to stop acting like buddy-pals and start acting like real enemies. Okay?

JAMES: Is this about the spies?

K: No dad, there are no spies.

JAMES: There *are* spies.

ANDREW: There are spies.

K: You tell me about spies, there *are no spies.* Is Andrew there?

ANDREW: Hi K!

K: Andrew, shut your mouth about the spies or I'll pull that Burger King crown around your fat, bald head!

JAMES: I am perfectly capable of examining the facts and drawing my own conclusions.

K: I wish there *were* spies, someone to watch the commercials and light the goddam switch board.

SPENCE: You're talking to Andrew?

K: I could *take a shit* with ceremonial, ritualistic purpose knowing there were red-eyed spies crouched in front of green screens peering at my fucking *upshot.*

JAMES: Upshot, what is that?

ANDREW: It's when the camera is positioned underneath the...

JAMES: I know. I know. I know.

K: Point is: No spies.

JAMES: Point is: Fix your hair.

ANDREW: Find your purse.

K: My hair looks great.

> *K mouths the question 'Is it bad?' to SPENCE. He nods 'Yes'.*

JAMES: You look like a tart.

K: Fuck you dad, powder your nose.

JAMES: Young Lady: you question my undying love and usher doubt inviting hate?

K: No dad, I cast a skeptical net and what I catch I throw back. Remember?
It's enough to have battled the fish and won,
we need not fry and feast to know in our hearts he be bested,
stricken momentarily from the food chain and returned quickly with scars and missing pride.
Trust me sir,
a fish with no pride dreams fondly of the pan.

JAMES: Why do you want to hurt me so?

K: I don't want to hurt you dad, but don't deny me my shame. Without shame I'd have no reason to keep my mind on other things.

JAMES: I'll be watching you during the commercials.

K: Good night dad. Best of luck. (*Hangs up.*) Old Whore.

JAMES: Little Twat.

SPENCE: Heart-warming!

K: What's the time?

SPENCE: It's that time.

3

JAMES: Can I have my Rubik's Cube?

ANDREW: No dice. We've got to do your object permanence tests.

K: Spence, can we skip it tonight? I don't need the aggravation.

SPENCE: Absolutely not, these tests are our only weapon against your crippling disease.

JAMES: Will I get to play with my Rubik's Cube afterward?

ANDREW: I will give you your Rubik's Cube and the home team advantage, you give me five minutes.

K: You're going to be reincarnated as a flip-flop.

SPENCE: That's hilarious. Juice boxes or teddy bears?

JAMES: Juice boxes.

SPENCE / ANDREW: Okay.

SPENCE and ANDREW stand and pull out small juice boxes and clipboards. JAMES and K massage their temples and squeeze their eyes shut.

K / JAMES: (*To themselves.*) Things exist when I can't see them. Things exist when I can't see them. Things exist when I can't see them.

ANDREW: Okay James. What do *you* think is inside this juice box?

SPENCE: Okay K. Why don't you go ahead and tell me what *you* think is inside this juice box.

K: Okay, let me stop you there. Is this a trick?

SPENCE: No. Please try to arrive at the most logical conclusion.

JAMES: Did you talk to Dr. Travis John about my results last week?

ANDREW: I reported your results and according to Dr. John you and K are functioning at the same level. Would you please concentrate Jim?

K: I'm really not functioning at my peak tonight Spence, can we postpone please?

SPENCE: Life is Eden but for the things required of us.

ANDREW: Please tell me what you think is inside this juice box.

Long Pause.

K / JAMES: Juice.

Simultaneously, SPENCE and ANDREW open the bottoms of the juice boxes and pull out a mess of red yarn.

JAMES: You tricked me.

SPENCE: Okay. What was *actually* inside the juice box?

ANDREW: You go ahead then tell me what was *actually* inside the juice box, okay James?

K / JAMES: Yarn.

SPENCE / ANDREW: Yarn, that's right! Very good.

JAMES and K smile.

SPENCE: Now, this is the hard part.

ANDREW: So concentrate.

SPENCE: *Before* I opened the juice box, what did you think was inside?

Long pause.

K / JAMES: Yarn?

SPENCE and ANDREW make a notation on their clip-boards.

K: Okay, Okay, I'm getting REALLY uncomfortable.

SPENCE: We're not done.

ANDREW: If I invited Susan, from down the hall, into this room.

JAMES: Okay, so Susan is in the room.

ANDREW: I invite her into the room.

JAMES: Shoot.

SPENCE: And I show her this juice box.

K: Okay.

SPENCE: What would Susan most likely guess, is inside this box?

Long Pause.

K / JAMES: Yarn?

SPENCE and ANDREW make a notation on their clip-boards.

K / JAMES: Son-of-a-BITCH!

SPENCE: The SAL News Organization and its parent company SALVON INDUSTRIES does not discriminate based on race, gender, age, sexual orientation, or disability.

ANDREW: Having established beyond a reasonable doubt our commitment to tolerance and diversity we ask that you: James Mann.

SPENCE: Katherine Feek Mann.

ANDREW: Undergo the necessary treatment and therapy to correct this unique, yet devastating psycho-developmental anomaly.

SPENCE: Though we appreciate the positive effect your complete and total lack of object permanence has on your nightly broadcast, we believe this inability to distinguish between your consciousness and the consciousness of others poses a major managerial problem and renders group-problem-solving strategies virtually useless.

ANDREW: Further, from an insurance perspective, it would be in our best interests if you were able to learn that objects which you cannot see are, in fact, still there.

JAMES: Andrew?

ANDREW: I'm right here.

JAMES: Oh. Okay.

SPENCE: Thank you for your continued cooperation with this humiliating court-ordered testing. That is all.

K: All right. I've got an appointment to invent.

JAMES: Can I have my Rubik's Cube?

ANDREW: Yes James.

SPENCE: K, we need to do some prep in editing.

K: Anytime, Anyplace, Anytime.

4

K: Which tape is this?

SPENCE: This is the 'Search for Atlantis' footage.

K: Did we have enough to create tension?

SPENCE: We've got fish swimming at the camera, that's our major visual pay-off and we've got...

K: Probably have to use that in the promo...

SPENCE: ...so it can't be the pay-off.

K: What's the pay-off?

SPENCE: We could fiddle with the diving footage, cut together, like, a tense possible drowning. Maybe Mario.

K: Which is Mario?

SPENCE: The pecs.

K: Okay, do we have any, like, 'scared to go down below' stuff that we can cliff-hang at the forty minute mark?

SPENCE: Um...we've got some 'mother died recently' stuff on him, but no real apprehension.

K: No seemingly naïve yet ultimately telling voodoo warnings?

SPENCE: Like: 'I can go no further'?

K: Right.

SPENCE: No.

K: And I'm just assuming there's no treasure.

SPENCE: No treasure.

K: And the diving tension would have to be manufactured?

SPENCE: Jump cuts and cellos.

K: Forget it then, bag it, sell it to National Geographic.

SPENCE: They wouldn't take it, the underwater cameraman didn't meter for the reefs.

K: Bag it, it's worthless.

SPENCE: I could edit a piece.

K: I don't have a very active imagination, if a story slaps me it should leave a handprint or less offensive words to that effect.

SPENCE: Fine.

K: Do we have the 'harming thoughts' piece done?

SPENCE: Basically, wanna see the intro?

K: Give it. 'A ride to the grocery store. A day in the park with your child.'

SPENCE: Hold on, let me run the music so you get a feel for it.

K: (*To self.*) 'A ride to the grocery store. A day in the park with your child.'

SPENCE: Okay five, four, three, two, one.

K: 'A ride to the grocery store. A day with your child at the...' shit.

SPENCE: Christ I JUST gave it to you don't have to try to memorize it.

K: Fine, I'll read it, I'm just trying to...

SPENCE: You don't have to show off for me like *I* could memorize it...

K: I'm not showing...for you? No, I mess up in front of you cause it doesn't mean anything, it's like doing it for a hamster.

SPENCE: Fine, just follow the words with your finger five, four, three...

K: Great job with Atlantis.

SPENCE: Fine, *sound it out* mush mouth five, four, three, two, one:

K: Kiss a dirty kitten.
'A ride to the grocery store.
A day in the park with your child.
The simple, perfunctory pleasures of a normal life.
Now imagine these simple tasks provoking in you not pleasure,
but heart-stopping fear and crippling trepidation.
Well, for thousands of Americans with OCD,
or obsessive-compulsive disorder,
this is an everyday reality.
Watch now as Cindy takes us inside the...' What is this?

SPENCE: What?

K: The carnival of phobia?

SPENCE: LOOK, the, shit, the opening shot is of the mother and daughter at a carnival.

K: No, that stinks. What am I? Vincent Price? 'The carnival?' It's very literal and I don't like it.

SPENCE: Well?

K: Takes us inside... 'the'... 'mind of'... 'chaos of the'... 'takes us inside the Cage of Thought'?

SPENCE: Who do you think you are?

K: Oh, I'm sorry: 'The Carnival of Thought.' What...is it brain-related?

SPENCE: What...the disease?

K: Yeah.

SPENCE: Yeah, they've got cat scans on it.

K: Takes us inside the... 'the compulsive mind'.

SPENCE: Fine.

K: Yeah?

SPENCE: How about 'inside the phobic mind'?

K: I don't like phobic, how about 'inside the Politics of Hesitation'?

SPENCE: How about just 'tricks of the mind'?

K: 'Inside the compulsive mind.'

SPENCE: Fine.

K: 'as she examines loosely-goosey goosey hand-washers who think they run over imaginary children in their cars.'

SPENCE: Great.

5

ANDREW: (*Checks his watch.*) James, would you like to see a photograph of K engaged in sexual activity?

JAMES: 'Who knows the depths to which dogs will sink to scrape the scraps from a wet bone? Who knows the untold distances traveled in pursuit of white hot experience?'

ANDREW: Are you positive?

JAMES: 'The baths of cash into which fools will leap diving for diamonds?'

ANDREW: I don't have a sense of humor.
I have a photograph of K engaged in some kind of sex act.

JAMES: Am I leading with...um...what is this, Anthrax?

ANDREW: October 13th, 2001. Tell me you don't want to see the photo and I'll throw it away.

JAMES: 'The countless stones tossed at prophets who dare alter the geography of the profit margin. The love of young girls enjoyed by men. The love of young boys enjoyed by men...'

ANDREW: We're talking HOTT here

JAMES: 'The glitter violence practiced by masked men and the rude faces they conceal.'

ANDREW: Last chance.

JAMES: 'Who knows the deep measureless sorrow of a cold world gone freezing?'

ANDREW: (*As if counting down.*) One.

JAMES: What kind of choice is this?

ANDREW shows JAMES the photo.

JAMES: AH. AH. No.

JAMES covers his eyes briefly. Then peeks. Then nearly has a heart attack. Then pretends he didn't see. Then perhaps gags.

ANDREW: We're going to lead with the Anthrax. It's a poison.

6

SPENCE: We've got about five minutes. Can I lube up?

K: Yeah. Hold on: 'American men, many of them bald, overweight, inarticulate, at the same time successful.'

SPENCE: Was there something about them being white?

SPENCE is rubbing sexual lubricant all over his neck.

K: If there was I didn't see it.

SPENCE: Me neither. Can we please?

K: Give me the tube.

K stands behind him and lovingly wraps a clear rubber tube around his neck, tightens it to cut off his oxygen.

The burden of power.

ANDREW: Should I put K on the monitor?

JAMES: Show me not your lustful chest.

K: You make me so tired Spence.

JAMES: Show me not your spit and tongue.

K: Every day I'm required to articulate my desires.

JAMES: Conceal your moaning thrusts.

K: I've got to put it in my own words.

JAMES: And spare your father the psychotic shame of a daughter's perversion revealed.

K: I'm tired of the sound of my own voice.

She releases him.

SPENCE: You're just tired.

K: I'm tired of using my imagination.

SPENCE: Use your oven.

K: I'm tired of your kitchen fantasies. 'Down on your knees with a soapy rag and a leather apron.'

SPENCE: I think it was a sponge.

K: In the kitchen I don't make car payments.

SPENCE: I didn't say kitchen K, I said oven. Insert head.

K: You'd love to come home to a tragic suicide.

SPENCE: Two minutes.

ANDREW: Five minutes Jim.

JAMES: On your knees my heart disowns you.
making this, your private dance,
all the more repulsive.
I stood before kings and tyrants
wearing nice suits.

SPENCE: I'm not so crazy about your hair tonight.

JAMES: Tin microphone in one hand. Neutral humility in the other.

ANDREW: It's not so bad Jim. Now you know she's not a dyke.

K: You're a lot like my father. I wish you would die.

SPENCE: Ten seconds. Nine. Eight. Seven.

K: Oh right, this is where I become an objective cyborg and eroticize the exchange of information. Now I remember.

7

SPENCE: ROLL INTRO!

K's Nightly News Broadcast music swells.

K: Good Evening, I'm K Mann. The Arctic Tundra: cold, lifeless, barren, highly reflective. Its terrain lives large in the imaginations of travelers and poets alike. The existentialists liken its unchanging landscape to the vast expanse of the modern mind. The surrealists have been known to draw inspiration from its optic density. The Arctic tundra: our exotic, freezing consciousness, now, in the year 2001, threatened by global warming, volcanic irregularity, ash storms, hot flashes, the thumping orgy of transnational industry.
Indeed:
We are the hot bodies which disturb this cold bed.
Is there a solution to this ecological meltdown?
Travis John has our report.

SPENCE: CLEAR. Ninety seconds K.

JAMES: Hot bodies indeed.

K: Turn my dad on. I want to watch.

ANDREW: Jim. Fifteen Seconds.

JAMES: Fifteen seconds!?

ANDREW: Well, you've been sitting there moping for ten minutes. K just finished her intro.

JAMES: You are my PERSONAL ASSISTANT!

ANDREW: Counting down from TEN. NINE. EIGHT. SEVEN.

JAMES: Fine. We're going to win this thing. You hear me? We're going to win this thing. I am the most trusted man in AMERICA!!

8

ANDREW: ROLL INTRO.

JAMES' World News Tonight music swells.

JAMES: Good Evening.
This is World News Tonight.
I'm James Mann.
Drugs:
Companies make them.
You take them.
Who's complaining?
The answer is:
Some people.
Some people think you're paying to much for your
prescription medication.
We've asked Dr. John Form, chief resident at
Philadelphia Medical and co-chair of the ACCP
to speak with us this evening.
Dr. Form?

DR. JOHN FORM (ANDREW): It's a pleasure to be here
James.

JAMES: Doctor, let's get down to the nitty gritty, shall we?
We could sit here and spar all day
but I don't think we'd get any closer to the naked truth.
And I think you agree
that's what the American people want.
It's what they deserve.
So let's take the gloves off,
if that's all right with you.

DR. JOHN FORM: That's what I'm here for Jim.

K: What is he doing? I hate this crap.

SPENCE: He's so 'direct'.

JAMES: Doctor, are we any closer to Universal Health
Care?

DR. JOHN FORM: We are no closer than we were twenty years ago.

JAMES: And we're not talking about Scary Joe Backstreet pushing barbs and alley juice in the parking lot, am I right? We're talking about multi-billion dollar corporations here.

DR. JOHN FORM: Yes.

JAMES: It might *seem* like a shakedown, yes? But this isn't a nickel and dime Hash and Dust racket is it?

DR. JOHN FORM: No.

JAMES: All right Doctor:

SPENCE: 30 seconds K.

K: Damn it.

JAMES: Doctor, you may be able to prescribe fancy drugs,
you can put your name down on the forms,
you can point to an x-ray and tell me about pain,
but doctor, these people live with the pain,
they can't turn it off,
you go home at night,
these people don't have that luxury.

K: He's totally lost it.

SPENCE: Ten seconds. (*Alarm sounds.*) Wait. Wait.

DR. JOHN FORM: What are you referring to?

SPENCE: We've actually got a breaking news story.

K: A what? What is this? A Superman comic?

SPENCE: We need another thirty seconds. Larry, give me a Snapple commercial!

JAMES: Well doctor, there are certainly a lot of lives at stake. We won't settle this tonight.

K: Let's not wait Spence... I want to scoop Dad. What is it?

SPENCE: Hold on. My printer is out of ink.

JAMES: Hold on. Doctor, I'm going to have to cut this short.

K / SPENCE: No NO NO NO NO NO.

JAMES: We have a breaking story. Please bear with me.

K: He got it. What else could it be? He scooped us.

SPENCE: Well, he's on the air!

K: WELL PUT US ON FUCKING THE AIR!

SPENCE: I ran the Snapple commercial.

K: SNAPPLE SUCKS!

JAMES: Dear God, ladies and gentlemen. This just in, a brave and well-organized act of violent protest against the systems of global capitalism has been executed in a major city by a group of disenfranchised theological radicals. I think we're going to cut to live pictures from New York.

K: That's it? That's the breaking story?

SPENCE: Ten seconds.

K: Do you have the copy?

SPENCE: I don't have anything. You just heard the story. IMPROVISE!

K: I can't improvise the news.

SPENCE: Then fucking PARAPHRASE. FIVE. FOUR. THREE. Fix your hair.

K: I am trying to report a tragic event!

SPENCE: Are we saying 'tragic?'

K: Ladies and gentlemen, this just in: details are sketchy at this point but our sources tell us a brave and well-organized act of violent protest against the systems of global capitalism has been... (*SPENCE hands her a piece of paper.*) ...hold on...a terrible tragedy has occurred in New York this evening...we're receiving conflicting reports.

JAMES: Ladies and gentleman, it appears pictures speak louder than words. Earlier reports underestimated the seriousness of this event. What you see on your screen is a horrifying landscape of chaos and devastation.

K: This was a senseless and cowardly act of violence against the people of New York. Looking at these pictures, it appears this might be the worst act of domestic terrorism in our nation's history. I might be wrong about that. Uh. (*Pause.*) Pearl Harbor was, of course...

JAMES: How bad was Pearl Harbor?

SPENCE / ANDREW: This is worse.

K / JAMES: We are witnessing *the worst* act of domestic terrorism in our nation's history.

9

A sudden blackout. SPENCE and ANDREW rummage for flashlights and eventually turn them on. It is the only light.

K: What is this?

SPENCE: Oh Christ. Power out.

JAMES: What, did the fucking plane hit our building?

K: Are we on the air?

SPENCE: No.

K: Is James on the air?

SPENCE: Uhhhhh, no.

K: Thank God.

JAMES: Andrew, did I sound distraught enough?

ANDREW: I don't know about distraught. You sounded pretty vigilant.

JAMES: Vigilant is good.

ANDREW: Vigilant is very good.

K: Get my dad on the phone.

SPENCE: The power could come back on.

K: I'm guessing it won't. Get my dad on the phone.

SPENCE dials. ANDREW picks up the phone.

ANDREW: AH HA! Who is it who calls ME? Who is it who utters my familiar name and beckons me to famous toil and empty performance?

SPENCE: Jesus Christ Andrew. I hardly think this is the time.

ANDREW: Right. Jim. It's Spence with K on the line.

SPENCE: Fucking pussy.

JAMES: Hey kid. You all right?

K: Oh yeah, I'm fine, we're just lighting a few hundred candles. You?

JAMES: This will all blow over.

K: Or it'll just blow up on national television.

JAMES: Yeah. No doubt 'heroes will emerge'.

SPENCE: 'Faster than a speeding bullet.'

K: 'Able to leap tall buildings in a single bound.'

JAMES: Well, some tall buildings aren't as tall as they used to be.

K: Let's take a field trip. I'll bunny hop over some 'tragic-looking debris'.

SPENCE: All-American hero.

ANDREW: The Real Target is Happiness.

JAMES: Pardon?

SPENCE: Hear that? Another gem from Andrew.

K: Dad, why do you let that mongoloid listen to our conversations.

JAMES: Because he's next in line for the throne.

SPENCE: What an honor.

ANDREW: Better than licking twat for pennies.

SPENCE: Kiss a Dirty Kitten.

ANDREW: Shut your mouth dirty.

K: So much for our little ratings war tonight. Duty calls.

JAMES: I don't know what you're talking about young lady. I'm certainly checking the overnight ratings.

K: Well OF COURSE I'm checking them. (*To SPENCE.*) Check the goddam ratings.

SPENCE: We're still technically on the air.

JAMES: There couldn't be a better test really. See who the American people turn to in a time of tragedy.

Alarm sounds.

ANDREW: This just in: We've officially declared war.

SPENCE: Oh shit. He's right.

JAMES: You hear that? How many *wars* have you covered sweet-heart?

K: Hang up on him would you?

JAMES: No *really*. Help me understand. Why would any sensible American coach potato turn to you for hard news? No one wants to hear about death counts and insertion techniques from a TART.

SPENCE: That's where you're wrong.

K: A tart?

JAMES: Yes A TART. You're a tarted up little tart and I can't stand to look at you (*Glancing at the picture that is still on his desk.*) from any angle.

K: That's a terrible lie.

JAMES: It's not a lie. You're *the* tart. The biggest tart. You're a national monument to the size and scale of all things tart.

K: Dad, you're very old and I can't make heads or tails of anything you're saying.

JAMES: Well, someone made heads and tails of you very recently. (*To ANDREW, pointing to the picture.*) Is that Spence?

K: Well, you've tried to embarrass me. Wasn't that easy?

JAMES: Terribly. 'Easy like sunday morning.' I'm going to BURY YOU in the overnights. And to think I was planning to retire.

K: Oh please dad. You'd actually deny us your diaper-load of nightly journalism? You're not even a newsman anymore, you're a pundit.

JAMES: This is a sign. Your time-slot change. The tragic events of five minutes ago. The war. I will make my mark.

K: A wet spot on the chair.

JAMES: I will make my mark. I will make my mark, and if I write it in the snow with piss, or on paper with blood, or drive my tank through lava and make fossils, this mark, my mark: It will be seen. Not by lousy people who might, if they are lucky, carry it as a memory for fifty or sixty years. My mark will live in the blood, like a partner to fear. How does that sound to you? People think I'm the nation's occasionally disturbing bedtime story. American's trusted newsman. But I am more. I will be a poison. A roadblock between feed and shit, between information and aneurysm. You don't have the balls or the battle scars to rock a nation to sleep every night.

K: Battle scars? Don't you mean paper-cuts?

JAMES: Hang up the goddam phone.

ANDREW hangs up.

I remember when she was a ten year old gluey.

SPENCE / ANDREW: This just in.

K: What now?

SPENCE: We won the war.

JAMES: Which war?

ANDREW: This one.

JAMES: The one from two minutes ago?

SPENCE: It was a black-tie knife fight.

ANDREW: Towel-heads surrender to scarecrows.

SPENCE: Use the words 'Superior Fire Power'.

JAMES: It's OVER?

ANDREW: The Ugly Souls of Heroes and Saints.

SPENCE: The Sneering Irony of Imaginary Accents.

ANDREW: The Real Target was Happiness.

K: Well, that's a lucky break.

Lights comes on.

10

JAMES: Oh perfect. What time is it?

ANDREW: Seven twenty eight. You've got time for a wrap-up.

K: Color me bad.

SPENCE: You're live in ten seconds.

K: So: They blew up our shit. We declared war. Some other shit happened. They surrendered. Let freedom ring: Correct?

SPENCE: The long and short.

K: No problem.

SPENCE: Can you squeeze out a tear?

K: So I can read about my breakdown in *Time* magazine? I'll stick with 'cold bitch'.

SPENCE: Live in five.

JAMES: Are we ready?

SPENCE: ROLL INTRO!

K's Nightly News Broadcast music swells.

K: Ladies and gentlemen: Welcome back. We've had some technical trouble here in New York related to the tragic events of ten minutes ago. I speak to you now, live, and listen carefully: All is well.

Pause.

Though pundits, cranks, and Luddites may occasionally bemoan the loss of American innocence, the treacherous pace at which we race towards our future, and the inevitable extinction of old-world craftsmanship: Tonight we might rejoice in our accelerated existence. Though communications were crippled momentarily, our military brought this ugly affair to a swift and satisfactory conclusion. War was declared, and war was won. Tonight, while we celebrate victory, let us not forget the lives lost in this terrible conflict. This is K Mann. Stayed tuned for 'Primeline'. Good night.

SPENCE: Clear!

JAMES: What was that?

ANDREW: That was quick and dirty. We're live in five.

JAMES: Who knows the depths to which dogs will sink to scrape the scraps from a wet bone?

ANDREW: Lets find out: ROLL INTRO!

JAMES' World News Tonight music swells.

JAMES: Good evening. I'm James Mann, returning to you now, as a shocked nation breathes a sigh of relief. Blink and you might have missed it: Thousands dead. Darkness. And then a light brigade visited revenge upon the dark hordes: recovering American dignity, demonstrating American courage. Conflict resolved.

Terrible things happen to terrible people in movies, but in life they are called VIP. Red ropes are no barrier, money: no object. Advice on how to spot a hero: blockhead says 'Anyone would have done what I did' and you've no hero on your hands. Just some selfish bum whose tornado of self-preservation carried a few cows. The real heroes labor in uncool little corners. Burn bright then disappear into darkness, or go home and make dinner. Villains? They own the rights to the X and Y chromosome. You can't spit without hitting a bad guy; the sun rises for them.

Let us remain vigilant, steel-eyed. Our convictions require a course of action. Was this a victory? For some. A cause for celebration? For some. If our sickness was blindness, complacency, let the events of this evening be a cure. I'm James Mann. Good night. Be well.

ANDREW: And we're CLEAR.

K: What a DOWNER!

SPENCE: Oh, he TOTALLY BOMBED.

ANDREW: I think that went well.

JAMES: I think I just fucked the family dog but thanks for the kind words.

ANDREW: Are we waiting for the overnight ratings?

K: I'm waiting.

JAMES: You can go.

SPENCE / ANDREW: I'll stay.

Blackout.

11

Lights up. K's hair is down. JAMES' tie is loose and he's drinking scotch. SPENCE and ANDREW look at their watches.

SPENCE: Shouldn't be long.

ANDREW: Must be stuck in traffic.

K: I should call that chump. He knows he's whipped.

SPENCE: He's your father.

K: How boring.

SPENCE: Why don't you stick a pitchfork between my ribs, twist till in pops, and don't stop twisting till you hear running water and my ghost whispering profanity in your ear.

K: Oh, you're planning to haunt me?

SPENCE: You scratch my back, I'll scratch yours.

K: I think I'll outlive you Spence. You don't have as many enemies dropping to their knees every night, begging the services of history's greatest assassin.

SPENCE: I have enemies.

K: You have lazy stalkers. They only turn up once a year to see if you changed your phone number.

SPENCE: They'll call.

K: Give 'em your cell.

SPENCE: I've got you: The prime time slut.

K: Who me? I'm a virgin.

SPENCE: No you aren't.

K: I'm a simulated virgin.

SPENCE: You're a vaginally-oriented virgin.

K: Do you mind?

JAMES: There aren't enough choices in this life.
Too often a man must blind himself to the dull similarities.
The crushing homogeny of the ever-present 'either/or.'
Like the choice between Coke and Pepsi.
So sharpened have our senses been,
by the cancer of similarity,
that we can truly 'taste the difference'.
So unlike a starving race are we,
the blinders on our eyes make our mouths water.

Like sick pigs,
our gluttony is a smiling suicide.
We can't tell the difference between the spear in our side,
and the slop in our mouth.
It's all classed as consumption.
Our body may appear solid but it is an orifice,
a feeding hole which man has trained himself to see,
and I am no better than this.
The true option frightens me,
give me false hope instead.
I'd rather pretend that Coke versus Pepsi is a choice,
than die from thirst,
wasted,
asking myself why I rocked the boat,
and risked falling into an empty pool.

ANDREW: When you smile like that you remind me of
someone.

JAMES: Hm. James Mason?

ANDREW: No.

JAMES: Are you sure it's not James Mason?

ANDREW: I'm sure.

JAMES: Paul Newman?

ANDREW: The chicken guy.

JAMES: Paul Newman had magnificent knuckles.

ANDREW: Colonel Sanders.

JAMES: Prison rock knuckles.
    Dipped in gold.
    He's easy on the eyes.
    So many actors.
    So much greasepaint.
    Countless broken legs.
    He's easy on the eyes.

Now me?
I'm just a high definition video star.
What time is it?

SPENCE: Let me check with Larry.

ANDREW: I think this is it.

K: Oh no.

SPENCE and ANDREW have both received the overnight ratings.

JAMES: These are just the major market ratings?

ANDREW: Yes.

K: It's too early for nationals?

SPENCE: Right.

JAMES: I would like to pray.

ANDREW: But I've already got them.

JAMES: Let us pray.

K: I bet dad is praying.

SPENCE: He better pray.

K: Are you serious?

SPENCE: As a heart-attack. You did it. You creamed him.

K grabs the ratings. She has beaten JAMES.

JAMES: Lord: You've blessed me with a long and successful career.

ANDREW: Jim. I'm holding the ratings.

JAMES: It DOESN'T MATTER!

ANDREW: Well what? Are they going to mysteriously change before my eyes?

JAMES: Bless the scars on the tops of our heads and the cuts on the bottoms of our feet Lord. Lord. God bless the fishnets. God bless hot loaves from the oven. God bless buns in the oven. God bless the twin trout and the troubled forest of sin.

ANDREW: You lost.

JAMES grabs the paper from his hands.

K: All right. Let's get him on the phone.

SPENCE: Okay. (*He dials.*)

12

ANDREW: What's up flap-jack?

SPENCE: Our ratings. Put James on.

ANDREW: Temporary set-back.

SPENCE: Yeah. Your hair-line. Put James on.

JAMES: Hey kid. Did you find your purse?

K: Aren't you proud of your daughter?

JAMES: Very proud. Listen now:

K: I was just writing your network eulogy. How's this sound: 'Do we live in a world of Salvon? A world of serious nonsense and half-hearted tragedy?'

JAMES: I'm retiring.

K: Quitter.

JAMES: I'm quite serious.

K: No really dad, it's no big deal. We go to war for ten minutes and America turns to her favorite foxy tart. I'm sure you'll bounce right back.

JAMES: I've no intention of bouncing or balling. I'm
    quitting.

K: So?

JAMES: So I wondered if you'll like to take over for me?

Pause.

K: How do you mean?

JAMES: I mean become the anchor of World News Tonight.
    Leave SAL. Take over my program.

SPENCE: Aren't you forgetting something Jim?

JAMES: KISS A DIRTY KITTEN.

SPENCE: K doesn't know the secret handshake. She can't
    work for VON.

ANDREW: Neither can you.

JAMES: I would, of course, sponsor her for The Cult of
    Weakness and Testimony.

K: Oh...you'd SPONSOR me. Fantastic.

JAMES: I can sponsor new members!

K: Who cares? I want no part of it.

SPENCE: Forget it.

K: Forget it!

JAMES: Now listen kid, my arms are wide open.

K: Let me peek up your sleeves.

JAMES: I can't believe what I'm hearing. The surging
    sounds of a brutal medieval memory. Screaming women
    and clicking iron!

K: I'm not going to join your little clan of the cave bear.

JAMES: It's not a clan of the...

K: It's a sad Masonic circle-jerk from your days at the Ivy League.

JAMES: It's a respectable social club!

K: It's an old-man-whiskey-perv-fest, you didn't allow women until 1992!

JAMES: It was 1989!

K: That wasn't a woman!

JAMES: I'll have you know she tested negative for...

K: Stop it. Stop it. You didn't want me when I was at Harvard and you won't get me now that I bring in more revenue than you.

JAMES: You watch your mouth. My program has a loyal following!

K: YES! That's right! It's a 'PROGRAM'!

JAMES: We are loyal to our sponsors!

K: I'd like to see how you'd float as a debut.

SPENCE: Yeah, we'd like to see how you'd float as a debut.

K: Yeah, without the Cult of Weakness and Testimony!

SPENCE: Yeah. Good luck.

JAMES: Is that Spence? Doesn't he have a job to do?

K: Oh, I'm sorry, you never slept with your editors?

SPENCE: HEY!

JAMES: A little self-respect!

K: Why? Why should he play by your rules? He'll never get into your little club.

SPENCE: I suppose I should fucking RETIRE.

ANDREW: Hear Hear!

SPENCE: Oh, congratulations Andrew, you filled their quota!

ANDREW: Hey champ I am three years older than you!

SPENCE: Yeah, I heard they just weaned you off VELCRO.

JAMES: Not so fast Spence. An empty space at the table is an empty space at the table.

SPENCE: Excuse me?

SPENCE is suddenly intrigued.

K: Oh bullshit.

JAMES: My only daughter? Don't you love me?

K: Oh come on dad.

JAMES: Tell me then. Tell how you love me.

K: No.

JAMES: No?

K: No.

JAMES: Well nothing will come of nothing. Speak.

K: I won't heave my heart into my mouth. I love your Majesty according to my bond, no more, no less.

JAMES: Listen to this.
Surrounded by loyalty and affection I turn again and again to the coldest heart.
Tell me why I am such a fool as to except abuse from mine own flesh and blood.
Tell me why I repeatedly turn my wounded ass toward your bloodied paddle.
I would demand an answer, but I've come to fear the moment your mouth opens.
A sixty-two year old man drowning in black bile, and every drop vomited by his own daughter!
Nothing comes of nothing. And you'll get nothing.

Andrew, hang up.

K: Suck my dick.

JAMES: FILTHY! FILTHY! Your ASS at the end of someone's TELE-PHOTO LENS!

K: Who's filthy? The one who begs his own daughter to sacrifice a career for the 'HONOR' of propping up your legacy? Get Andrew to suck your dick 'cause I don't know anyone else who will......

SPENCE 'karate chops' K and she passes out. Or maybe a 'Vulcan neck pinch'.

13

SPENCE: James? About that empty space at the table?

JAMES: Ah ha. You wanna join the club Spence?

SPENCE: Sir. I'm well aware of my own limitations and would NEVER advise you in such a important decision. I'm quite certain your heir will be the most qualified party, blood or none. I only ask that you forgive Katherine her insane indifference. It is born of pride and foolishness, maybe a bit of fatigue. Perhaps you'll allow me to speak on her behalf.

ANDREW: If it isn't the Duke of Burgundy?

SPENCE: Kiss a dirty kitten.

ANDREW: Oh to be young and insecure!
Tell me that what my eyes do see doth exist.
Pussy-whipped said the knave!
And that's not just my dirty mouth.
That's the truth observed and duly noted.
Your balls nailed to the uterine wall,
or maybe clipped?
Now we know Katherine fixes up real nice,
and sweats like a wet lemon.

You are her degenerate partner,
not her spokesman.

SPENCE: Were K in her right mind, or perhaps willing to
see the truth in *you* sir she might say: 'Sir, I love you
more than word can wield the matter. Dearer than
eyesight, space, and liberty.' Something like that.

JAMES: You want my job Spence? Want to join the Cult of
Weakness and Testimony?

SPENCE: Well Jim, I'm not sure you're offering.

JAMES: Are you sure? Think hard. Am I offering?

SPENCE: You're not offering?

JAMES: You don't want to join? You're too mature? Too
mature? Too cosmopolitan?

SPENCE: No sir.

JAMES: Maybe you aren't qualified?

SPENCE: Maybe I'm not.

JAMES: Not with that attitude. What happened to my
favorite pretentious snot-rag? You know how I acted
around my wife's father? When I was your age? I acted
like I was carrying Alaskan pipeline in my shorts. I was
a cocky bastard. I wanted him to think, every time he
saw me, that's the man who splits my daughter in half.

SPENCE: Well. Your talent eclipses my arrogance. I
thought sincerity might work...in this case.

JAMES: I'll think about it. For now, you're not invited. We
want news makers, not news writers. You're a soft-serve
ice-cream cone. Why don't you call me when you
replace those hangnails with some battle scars.

K wakes up.

K: You mean paper-cuts, right dad?

JAMES: Hang up Andrew. (*He does.*)

K: What happened?

SPENCE: You passed out. I don't know. Let's celebrate.

14

Lights on JAMES and ANDREW.

JAMES: 'Tis our fast intent to shake all cares and business from our age, conferring them on younger strengths while we Unburdened crawl toward death. World News Tonight with Katherine Mann.

ANDREW: Jim, your heir is neither strong nor young. Her weakness is sin, disorder, and disrespect, and age ain't nothin' but a number. Twenty-eight years and twice as many partners. She is Messalina covered in slime.

JAMES: She has a strong fan-base.

ANDREW: And a monkey will eat sand if you make him.

JAMES: What of her youthful glow?

ANDREW: She fucked it off. It sits like dry snakeskin underneath her desk.

JAMES: (*Sighs hard.*) Do you like working for me Andrew? Do you like straightening my tie and checking my spelling? Do like to hide in the bushes and snap photos of my perverse child? Does it bring you pleasure, to attend to this heroic fool with no object permanence, senile since birth and positively busting with wealth and barely-earned respect? Or are you disgusted by this big flap-jack?

ANDREW: I'm not disgusted. I admire and respect you. I consider it an honor and privilege to work alongside you. I profess myself an enemy to all other joys.

JAMES: I reported Vietnam.

They had underground tunnels.
The Vietnamese.
We never wrote about that.
But they were there.
They told us if we kissed a Vietcong woman
We'd be immune to the poisons of the jungle.
And if we killed one, we'd go straight to heaven.
War is hell.

ANDREW: Hell: War.

JAMES: Down there in the shit.

ANDREW: Hold on Jim, could you cover your ears?

JAMES: Why?

ANDREW: I'm going to do an aside.

JAMES: Oh, certainly.

ANDREW: That's the Swine Technique.
    Buy some mouthwash.
    He just fed you his favorite waste.
    Maybe Vietnam was just a very popular broadway show,
    and you met the heroic understudy,
    James Mann,
    our man in the field,
    always there in a pinch.
    Oh the sorrow!
    He was there when they dug the grave,
    developed the film,
    the human suffering.
    He lied to you.
    You bought it.
    Hit the showers.
    Jim?

JAMES: Huh?

ANDREW: Okay. I accept.

JAMES: Say what?

ANDREW: Though I will mourn alongside your many viewers, I accept your decision.

JAMES: My decision?

ANDREW: I agree with you. I've been warming the bench for too long. It is time to step up to the plate. I know I can never fill your shoes. That's not my role. But perhaps, just perhaps, I can sit in your chair, beneath your lights, and live out the rest of my days honoring you, doing my best James Mann impression. Unless you've changed your mind?

JAMES: No?

ANDREW: Did you forget?

JAMES: I didn't forget anything.

ANDREW: Perhaps you'd like a rematch with K? Following such a humiliating defeat I imagine you'd like to come out of retirement, go one last round in hopes of reclaiming your title. Tin microphone in one hand...

JAMES: ...neutral humility in the other.

ANDREW: Sure thing. Why not that? Were this your kingdom for a moment longer, or a decade, each moment would be a reward in and of itself. I can wait.

JAMES: Remind me now: What would you be waiting for?

ANDREW: To take over. World News Tonight. As your permanent substitute of course.

JAMES: Of course.

ANDREW: With you as executive producer.

JAMES: Naturally.

ANDREW: And Spence as my personal assistant.

JAMES: Spence?

ANDREW: Certainly you remember? His begging? His sniveling, insincere plea to serve you in any way possible? The startling revelations about his cock-size?

JAMES: Ahhhh…

ANDREW: You remember your daughter's disloyalty?

JAMES: YES! Oh I remember…

ANDREW: Good. Then we've settled. (*Presents a contract.*) Sign here.

JAMES signs the contract.

ANDREW: And the Wonderful Smell of Locker Rust.

JAMES signs again.

ANDREW: And the Final Word on Wall-to-Wall Virginity.

JAMES signs again.

ANDREW: And the Burning Branches of Family Tree.

JAMES signs away his job to ANDREW.

ANDREW: Cool. Remember what we talked about.

JAMES: I certainly will.

15

Lights on K and SPENCE.

K: The violation. You bust me, that's the verb. My cherry. The direct OBJECT.

SPENCE: I haven't been an intellectual for a long time.

K: It's a violation. You bust me, *that's* the verb. *My* cherry.

SPENCE: Are you having a fat day?

K: I'm just asking you to have a critical consciousness about our sex life.

SPENCE: Why?

K: 'Cause critical consciousnesses are hot.

SPENCE: I think you need your brain stroked. This is foreplay.

K: Which is more oppressive: language or biology?

SPENCE: Oh my god. Does language really confine you?

K: Yes it does confine me. Sex is the transgression of my physical body as I experience it through language.

SPENCE: Well, transgression is practically a synonym for orgasm.

K: You are totally misunderstanding me.

SPENCE: How?

K: I don't want any more of your transgression.

SPENCE: Whatever.

K: No really. It's all so planned and compartmentalized.

SPENCE: Fine. We'll fuck missionary from now on.

K: There are a million men who need to hear some smart slut coo the word masturbation.
You can't fire a gun without wounding some private pervert,
kind-hearted and well-intentioned,
but still hopelessly longing for some voyeur's eclipse,
the day he looks out his window and sees some hard-bodied virgin engaged in silent self-satisfaction.
You're the love test machine.

SPENCE: I'm a goddam sexual tyrannosaurus.

K: The love test machine.

Rate yourself as a lover one through ten.
How long can you last?
How big is it?
How many did she have?
Twelve ways to spice up your sex life.
Five things every guy should know.
Fourteen day cycles.
Sperm count.
G-spot.
The rhythm method.
Technique.
Minutes, seconds, inches, numbers, methods, charts, counts, cycles, spots, pills, packages, digits, decimals, pumps, PC muscles, CONTROL.
Orgasmic control? Orgasmic control?
What ever happened to train wreck sex?

SPENCE: Is this a take-down scene? Is that what we're doing here?

K: You think you're such a maverick, don't you? Such a champion. Colossal arrogance balanced with charming insecurity. So unconcerned with your body, so candid about your obsessions.

SPENCE: Don't forget un-ambitious.

K: Right. So attentive to my orgasms but so quick to play the part of the rapist. You're drowning in irony.

SPENCE: At least I'm not swimming in principle.

K: Am I principled?

SPENCE: No. No. You're totally unprincipled.

K: You're right. I should abandon this network.

SPENCE: Why not?

K: I should abandon *my* program because he cleared a space at the table for me?

SPENCE: A space? He cleared 'a space'? He cleared THE space. He asked you to be the anchor person.

K: This upsets you.

SPENCE: I just want to know why.

K: Why what?

SPENCE: Why deny him?

K: Him?

SPENCE: Not even him. YOU. Why deny yourself?

K: And tell him what he wants to hear?

SPENCE: YES. That's exactly what you do. You tell him what he wants to hear. You get the job. You cash the check, put a smile on his face before he dies, and win. You win everything.

K: Wait. You mean put a smile on YOUR face.

SPENCE: It would kill you. Just explain it to me. Why not take it? And don't tell me about being the 'first-woman' this and 'girl-power' that cause I KNOW you don't care about any of that. It's just a smoke screen to confuse a very old man.

K: I don't have to tell you. You ASSUME I've made the right decision. That's your job.

SPENCE: No. You DO have to tell me. 'Cause I don't understand.

K: Don't yell at me.

SPENCE: So you join Jim's little steam-room circle-jerk and make more industry connections than you could from years of hustling. You earn the right to be somber, the voice of reason...or if you want to be principled...you 'destroy the system from the inside' and change things. It'll do wonders for other girls, is that the problem?

K: Shut up.

SPENCE: Don't worry babe. You can shut the gate behind you, if that's what you want. It wouldn't be the first time.

K: I'm not joining. I could care less about my competition, let them join.

SPENCE: They would if they could. I WOULD if I could. It's a slap in the face.

K: I won't eat his garbage.

SPENCE: Why? I heard you and I'm still asking.

K: Because he's my father. And I refuse to sanction his weak-willed, desperate contribution to my life. They are OVERRATED. All the daddies. Overrated. Even you.

SPENCE: Very melodramatic.

K: Fine. It's melodramatic. I won't be a part of it.

SPENCE: You LOVE him. Christ, I see him in you EVERY day. You're exactly like him. You give orders like him. I can barely tell you apart. At your birthday party I didn't know whether to shake his hand or kiss him good night.

K: It's very funny.

SPENCE: Suddenly you're CRIPPLED by principle.

K: Do you have any idea how I feel about my father?

SPENCE: Yes.

K: You do?

SPENCE: Yes.

K: He loves me like cancer loves cells.
He wants to be a dark cloud.

He wouldn't save me from drowning unless it was him
that pushed me in.
Does that make sense to you?
He gives to take.
He kidnaps his own affection and holds it hostage.
Asks me for the ransom.

SPENCE: I think you're being dramatic.

K: There can be no genuine give-and-take between us.

SPENCE: He's your father, not your boss. You don't need
'give-and-take'.

K: Fuck him with tornados and lava.

SPENCE: If your mother heard you.

K: I hate my mother.

SPENCE: Jesus K, she gave birth to you.

K: It was cesarean.

SPENCE: You love him.

K: I love him dead. I love him senile. I will never love the
HIM in ME.

SPENCE: Mend your speech a little. Lest you may mar
your fortunes.

K: Mar my fortunes?
That I could erase my father's print from this flawed
heart.
That I could cut the cords of his which clutter my throat
and break the fingers which ape his echoed gestures.
God.
That I could rip his glowing seed from my soul and be
born again without the sick slime he hath passed onto
me.
Toxic waste which flows through my body excretes itself
involuntarily as words and deeds.

I believe I will never love as long as his blood pumps
my veins.
As long as his sour puss appears prior to each misstep
and regrettable failure.
They call me a hysteric, plagued with nonsense that I
might hold him responsible for each flaw but it is so.
He hath brought me into this world to ruin me.
Created from his own ash a slave with long invisible
chains which he may yank whenever his day is dark.
To cure my cancer I will make him beg to be forgiven.
I will feed and clothe him when he is too poor to do
these things himself.
I will keep him alive until he knows that my name is not
what he gave me,
but what *I carved from nothing.*
At his last moment I will dismiss this stranger with a
kiss,
pausing only to tongue his last cold tear.

SPENCE: You're a brat. A selfish, spoiled, perverted,
pretentious little brat tart flap-jack cunt. You're a whore
for independence.

K: I'm a professional.

SPENCE: Yeah, the world's oldest professional:
worthlessness.

K: *I'm* preparing myself for the loneliness of fame.
And the eventual inability to feel that loneliness.
And the gradual disappearance of my identity.
And the dread of facing what they replace it with.
I'm building a shelter for my hunted personality,
and trying to build a decoy,
before they build one for me,
out of my own flesh and blood,
paint a target on it,
and leave me to rot.

SPENCE: I'm your ally. I want what is best for you.

K: I'm not stupid. It's 'bros before hoes' with you.
You bitch.
Every back comes with a knife and no shortage of hands
to stab.

SPENCE: That's James.

K: What?

SPENCE: Your dad said that.

16

JAMES dials K's number. The phone rings several times.

K: Hello. You've reached Katherine Mann. I'm not available
to take your call at the moment. Please leave a message
and I'll get back to you.

JAMES: K. It's your father. It's four a.m. I think. I've
resigned my position at the network. Andrew has
handled the details of the replacement. I don't know. I
thought he was the Clark Kent to my Superman. Now I
think he's the Ronald Reagan to my crack mother.

Pause.

I'm going to tell you something now, hon, I hope you
appreciate my honesty and candor. I am an old man and
I flatter myself that I am distinguished, respected, I know
that I am rich, and with that comes certain privileges,
and certain responsibilities. In many ways I am not
unlike the family dog. At one time, it is some kind of
wolf, in danger of starving, until gradually over time, the
half starving wolf will enter a home and accept food in
exchange for changes in behavior. It accepts shelter and
gives a kind of love, but there are certain ugly details
which creep into this relationship as it develops –
castration, confinement, the licking of peanut butter from
women's genitals – which may appear to be parts to a
downside, but are in fact key to the cycles of pleasure
and power which do not necessarily exist in the day-to-

day but rather manifest themselves outside the established and visible parameters of society.

Pause.

I am a member of a cult. And you might think that joining the Cult of Weakness and Testimony is like being domesticated. Really it's nothing like that. It's quite nice. Maybe I sound crazy to you. OH MY GOD. Oh sorry, I thought I saw a mouse. What was I talking about? Anyway, good night.

JAMES hangs up. ANDREW dials. The phone rings.

SPENCE: Hi, this is Spencer. I'm not home. Leave me a message and I'll get back to when I get a chance.

ANDREW: Hey dirty dirty. Just calling to remind you that I will visit down upon you sewer rats, ripe with disease, yellow teeth snipping wildly around the edges of flesh for food. Rats: starving from lack of foam and dry-mouthed from proximity to the fires of hell. You need go no deeper than the sewer.

These animals, more insect than mammal, sooner to burn with acid blood than appear beautiful even in morning light, will fall from the sky until halted by your head and shoulders. There they will sit, hysterical red eyes blinking thoughtlessly, pulling at your hair, plucking each stalk from its greasy spool, ingesting the fiber, and in turn spilling forth a foul pile of waste upon your bald brain. Brain made bald by the fierce gnawing and ceaseless chewing. This is Andrew. Call me tomorrow before you pick up K.

ANDREW hangs up. K dials the phone. The phone rings.

SPENCE: Hi, this is Spencer. I'm not home. Leave me a message and I'll get back to when I get a chance.

K: Spence.
This is K.

I can't sleep.
I got a message from the credit card company.
The thieves. The ones who stole my wallet:
They bought an electric car.
Why don't you go ahead and cancel my credit cards
tomorrow.
And cancel my membership at the gym.
Cancel my grocery delivery service.
Cancel my electrolysis.
Close my Swiss bank account.
Sell my old underwear on eBay.
Empty my inbox. Change my password.
Clean out my mini-fridge.
I'm streamlining.
Not disappearing.
Cancel our engagement.
Clear my schedule.
I have an appointment to invent.

K hangs up. SPENCE dials the phone. The phone rings.

ANDREW: Is it recording? Hey, this is Andrew. Leave your
name and number and speak clearly. And I'll get back to
you. Bye. Okay is that it? How do I save that?

SPENCE: I got your message dirty dirty.
I'll meet you tomorrow before I pick up K.
I've got a present for you.
A desk-warming gift.
Very warm.

SPENCE hangs up.

17

*JAMES MANN'S office. JAMES is seated. K MANN, his daughter,
is combing his hair. ANDREW sits in JAMES' position for broadcast.*

JAMES: Do I live in a world of Salvon?
A world of serious nonsense and half-hearted tragedy?
An upside-down castle where yes is no and sex is

painful?
Or is my world simple to name?
Give it six letters moving left to right and it will be
ordered and neat.
Surrounded by lies, we twist in the wind.
Stop my teeth from chattering.

K: Sit still.

JAMES: I am a neutral fool, and the image I create is false
as teeth, white and straight.
Teeth, when hungry they tear, when vicious, they bite.
When aroused they click and break against the gates of
another.
That my teeth are fake, white and straight, precludes all
abandon.
Even my most passionate hunger is executed with hollow
precision and sterile agility.
Thank my bloodless teeth.

SPENCE: I'll have her in the car by six-forty-five. Stand by.

ANDREW: James. Shouldn't you be in the office?

JAMES: Fill me with your sour puss
Until I am milk-fed, fat as a baby
Replace my words with moans
and drown my brain in sex.

K: This better not be a cry for help.

SPENCE: K we've got five minutes.

K: Dude. SHUT. UP.

JAMES: I am a law-abiding citizen.

SPENCE: James. Don't you want to make a good
impression on your first day?

K: Do you hear that? That's your future.

JAMES: It's my sentence.

K: No more applause. Just giggles in the hallway.

JAMES: Who was it that sealed my fate?

SPENCE: K. The car is outside. What do you want me to do?

K: I want you to WAIT.

JAMES: Who gave me the cold shoulder?
Who gave me the hairy eye-ball?
Who tried to pass off a wooden nickel?
Who tried to get service with no shoes?

ANDREW: And no shirt.

K: Is this a speaker-phone system, or an intercom, or what?

JAMES: The grateful and loyal have been rewarded.

SPENCE: K. The car.

K: I'm don't care about Andrew! I'm worried about you.
You shouldn't retire. You shouldn't give your desk to that fucking chimp!

SPENCE: K. THE CAR.

ANDREW: I'm the son he never had.

K: You're the kitten he never drowned.

SPENCE: K!

K: Fuck this. Bring the fucking car.

ANDREW: James, there is stack of copy on your desk that needs to be attended to.

JAMES: You swear too much.

K: Good luck dad.

*K kisses his cheek. JAMES wipes his cheek. SPENCE wheels
K to her broadcast desk.*

JAMES: Cannibalism. It's an ugly word, an even uglier practice, and it might be more common than you think.

ANDREW: James!

JAMES: Huh?

ANDREW: Get to the office now!

JAMES looks around, then stands up and carries his chair over to ANDREW's assistant position and sits.

K: What have we got?

SPENCE: You're doing an interview with CNC.

K: When?

SPENCE: Thirty seconds. Look straight ahead.

K: What's the research?

SPENCE: It's a post-events-of-twenty-four-hours-ago commemoration to honor the heroes and raise money for the victims. We're just going to hit all the high-points: bravery of firemen, cowardliness of terrorists, where-were-you-when, ignoring the sweet sweet temptations of German philosophy, and your favorite food.

K: What about my vigilance?

SPENCE: You'll get a prompt about vigilance. Three, two one...

K: What about dad? Are they asking about dad?

TRAVIS JOHN (SPENCE): Good evening Mrs. Mann thank you for speaking with us.

K: Well, it's bittersweet.

TRAVIS JOHN: What's that?

K: My pleasure. The pleasure in being here, speaking with you, is bittersweet. That is, it's my bittersweet honor that you would ask me about my vigilance.

TRAVIS JOHN: Excuse me?

K: These are very confusing times. Overwhelming.

TRAVIS JOHN: Indeed.

K: I think we've all had our fill of vigilance.

ANDREW: Are you watching this?

JAMES: Makes sense to me.

TRAVIS JOHN: Our fill of vigilance?

K: Of everything really...we're all very overwhelmed, even those of us in the public eye, we're news persons, some might say news-victims, but we're just like everyone else. Victims. We're overdosing on terrorism and victory. It's exhausting really, thank you for contacting me I'd be more than happy to answer any of your questions.

TRAVIS JOHN: Well Ms. Mann. Last night's historic father-daughter stand-off...

K: It seems so far away now. Insignificant.

TRAVIS JOHN: Was interrupted by the tragic-events-of-twenty-three-hours-ago. You experienced a black-out.

K: We're just like everyone else, really. There is a tremendous sorrow.

TRAVIS JOHN: An overwhelming number of people turned to your program in these troubling...

K: Overwhelming times. Travis...

TRAVIS JOHN: Yet ultimately resolved.

K: The events yes, I reported on the resolution last evening. Following the blackout. We thought it was important to remain vigilant.

TRAVIS JOHN: Many are saying your words should be engraved in the...

K: Excuse me Travis, I'm going to need to cut this short.

TRAVIS JOHN: I'm not sure...

K: Travis I'm a professional and I get paid not to let it show.

TRAVIS JOHN: I'm sure we all understand. You're a human...

K: Thank you and good night.

ANDREW: CLEAR!

SPENCE: WHAT THE HELL WAS THAT???

K: Oh. My. God. I don't know.

ANDREW: This is perfect. She's cracking up.

SPENCE: That was totally horrible!

K: I know. I know. I know.

SPENCE: How am I supposed to spin that?

JAMES: She could spin it.

K: Oh shit. Um.

SPENCE: Technical difficulties?

K: No.

JAMES: Maybe she doesn't have to spin it.

ANDREW: She just cracked up.

JAMES: This is what you need to learn.

K: Wait. It's good.

SPENCE: It's not good.

ANDREW: Let's do the headlines.

K: I want to see the headlines.

JAMES: Are you sure that would be productive?

K / ANDREW: Productive?

SPENCE: Let me just read it out loud.

JAMES: *New York Times*: 'America Rises To The Challenge.'

K: Not the shit about the war.

ANDREW: The stuff about me.

SPENCE: Okay. *New York Times*: '4000 Dead. One Retires.'

JAMES: *Chicago Times*: 'James Mann Delivers Final Broadcast, Eulogy for American.'

K: Okay wait.

SPENCE: I know.

K: Dad retired at one a.m. last night.

SPENCE: I know.

K: How the hell did Andrew get it into the papers today?

SPENCE: I know.

JAMES: You moved pretty quick on this one Andrew.

ANDREW: What can I say. American loves you. Next.

SPENCE: *Washington Post*: 'The New Face of American Vigilance.'

K: Me or Andrew?

SPENCE: You baby!

K: That's what I'm talking about.

ANDREW: TOTAL BULLSHIT.

JAMES: Please take into consideration the Unfortunate Transparency of Pants and Dresses.

K: What else?

SPENCE: Ummmm. *Fox News*: 'K Mann, Born Again Hard.'

K: Republican horn-dogs.

JAMES: Here's something: *Chicago Sun Times*: 'The Most Trusted Voice in America Names a Successor.'

ANDREW: That's Peter at *The Sun*. He's a friend.

JAMES: 'A total unknown, Andrew Polackowski will be the first Polish-American news anchor...'

ANDREW: The NAME CHANGE! I FORGOT TO CHANGE MY NAME.

JAMES: Right. But if you changed your name they wouldn't have written: 'Andrew Polackowski will be the first Polish-American...'

ANDREW: I know.

SPENCE: I told him to change his name.

K: More.

SPENCE: 'The young unknown is expected to deliver a tribute to James Mann, followed by a lengthy montage of some of his greatest moments on the air.'

K: Cheese.

JAMES: Is this true?

ANDREW: Yeah. I'm going to do a whole thing about you at the top of the show. Peter is cutting together your greatest hits, and I'll need the heartwarming tribute on my desk by five.

JAMES: Greatest hits?

ANDREW: You know: The Korean War editorial.

SPENCE: Shooting cows from a helicopter in Vietnam.

K: The Kentucky Tornado of '78.

ANDREW: The John Hinkley Jr. Interview.

SPENCE: Buying crack undercover.

K: When George Bush punched you in the face.

ANDREW: Unearthing Liberace's Secret Vault.

SPENCE: The tragic events of twenty-six hours ago.

K: The tragic events of twenty-six hours ago.

ANDREW: So like I said if you could just whip up a short and dignified farewell to American's Favorite Occasionally Disturbing Bedtime Story that would be great.

K: Prediction: Andrew is going to monkey this up and it will be the first and last time anyone watches World News Tonight with Andrew Polackowski.

SPENCE: But they will be watching.

K: Oh yeah. Schedule a commercial break. I want to watch it too.

SPENCE: That would be perfect.

K: Get him on the phone.

SPENCE: Who?

K: Dad.

SPENCE: Okay.

ANDREW: How about 'Death Bed Letters: Correspondence From People Dying Of AIDS.'

JAMES: It should be: 'Death Bed Correspondence: Letters From People Living With AIDS.'

ANDREW: Right. Hold on. Hello?

SPENCE: What's new pussycat?

ANDREW: 'Janie's Got A Gun.'

SPENCE: I've got K on the line for James.

ANDREW: Oh hey, listen. Jimmy isn't supposed to take personal calls at the office. Sorry about that.

SPENCE: He says Jimmy isn't supposed to take personal calls at the office.

K: Andrew? Put dad on the phone and I promise not to fucking LIQUEFY you in the ratings tonight!

ANDREW: Hit me with your best shot there Benatar! I'm going to destroy you in the overnights.

K: Just remember to take the hanger out of your jacket.

ANDREW: Be careful you don't accidentally BUTTON YOUR BLOUSE before you go on national television.

K: Blouse? We're wearing shirts this season! PUT DAD ON THE PHONE!

ANDREW: It's K.

JAMES: Katherine?

K: Dad, I think you're well on your way to history's unmarked grave of discarded lies.

JAMES: Well, I'm going to start taking Prozac.

K: Do you know the joke about Prozac?

JAMES: What joke?

K: How do you get a prescription to Prozac?

JAMES: I don't know, how do you get a prescription to Prozac?

K: You either have to prove that you're depressed or prove that you're married.

JAMES: Good one.

K: You told me that.

JAMES: I did?

K: Dad. I want to congratulate you on your retirement. I want to wish you the best of luck shining that turd sitting in your desk. And I want to invite you to dinner tonight.

SPENCE / ANDREW: Heartwarming.

JAMES: Don't you have better things to do after dark?

K: Not anymore.

JAMES: Honored though I might be by this generous invitation, we remain enemies, locked in a petty struggle for network supremacy.

K: I call it a Victory at the Dirt Palace. The lowest kind of triumph. Destined to wash away with the sand.

SPENCE / ANDREW: Deep.

JAMES: I fear our tardy reconciliation may be in poor taste.

K: Well that's perfect. I don't have any taste. Just appetite.

JAMES: I'll pencil you in.

K: Salvon.

JAMES: Salvon.

SPENCE / ANDREW: Nauseating.

K: Can we run the Nazi role-playing piece?

SPENCE: No. It's time for your object permanence tests.

JAMES: Unbelievable.

K: Can we skip it tonight Spence? In memory of the victims of yesterday's terrible attacks?

SPENCE: Absolutely not. These tests are our only weapon against your crippling disease.

JAMES: But I'm your executive producer.

ANDREW: Juice boxes or teddy bears?

JAMES: Juice boxes.

SPENCE and ANDREW stand and pull out the juice boxes.

SPENCE / ANDREW: Okay.

ANDREW: What do you think is inside this juice box?

SPENCE: Why don't you go ahead and tell me what you think is inside this juice box.

JAMES: Let me stop you right there.

ANDREW: Okay.

JAMES: I might be drowning in chocolate pudding.

K: Give me a minute.

JAMES: My mind may be riddled with hot snakes and cold potato salad.

K: I'm going to take a minute to think.

JAMES: I may be defeated. Dethroned. Excommunicated. Tricked into reversing evolution. Pink slipped off the deep end. Downsized. Diaper-wrapped.

K: I remember the answer.

JAMES: There might even be a small merry-go-round in my skull that my brain rides twenty-four hours a day.

K: Memory is three-dimensional.

JAMES: But razor-blade tornadoes of VOMIT and RAT-SHIT couldn't force me to spend ONE MORE HUMILIATING MOMENT doing these tests!

K: Juice.

SPENCE pulls yarn out of the box.

JAMES: I don't need history. I don't need triangulated thought! I don't need object permanence.

SPENCE: Before I opened the juice box...what did you think was inside?

ANDREW: You need object permanence to do your job. You need to know that thing exist when you can't see them.

JAMES: To do what? The NEWS?

ANDREW: Yes.

K: I'm thinking.

JAMES: The news is just jokes. Familiar stories with memorable endings, twisted anecdotes. You want to know what's really going on, pull up a front line, grab a square foot of squalor, get shot, shoot up, absorb the guitar solo, send email. You know who *watches* the news? Same people check the menu in the window before they eat at the restaurant. I'M GOING TO BECOME A WEATHERMAN!

K: Juice.

K is correct. SPENCE is shocked.

JAMES: Give me weather prediction. From fiction to fact with an eighty-three percent chance of accuracy. I've got your doll boy, hide the pins.

SPENCE: That's right. Juice.

JAMES: Tornadoes can suck my dick I seen 'em comin'.

SPENCE: What? Are you suddenly cured?

K: I suppose.

ANDREW: THIS IS BULL CRAP. BULL CRAP. I'm trying to increase your quality of life. I'm trying to enrich your existence. I'm trying to carry on with your STUPID legacy so that this STUPID network doesn't go down the GD toilet! Okay champ? If you don't want to enrich your existence by developing the basic cognitive skills of a two and half year old child, and continue speaking in maddening mix of childish avant-english and cut-rate Shakespearean HORSE TWIDDLE, and forgive your whore daughter and keep brow beating me, WELL BE MY GUEST! Just BE MY GUEST!

JAMES: Jesus Polackowski pull yourself together. You're on in two minutes.

SPENCE: I don't know what to say.

K: I'm on in five minutes.

SPENCE: You're on in five minutes.

K: Great. Why don't you leave?

SPENCE: Leave?

K: Yeah. Go find a way to make my job easier.

SPENCE: I thought maybe you'd want to...before you go on.

K: Nah. Just put World News Tonight on the monitor tell me when it's my turn.

SPENCE: Maybe I should be quiet.

K: Maybe you should.

ANDREW: Two minutes.

JAMES: That's right. My tribute is on your desk.

ANDREW: Everyone loves an underdog. I think I'm going to surprise a lot of people tonight.

JAMES: No they don't. No you won't.

ANDREW: Right. It's just jokes.

JAMES: You're not an epic hero. You're a flexible character in an avant-drama.

ANDREW: I think I'm going to surprise a lot of people tonight.

JAMES: Relax your shoulders. You look like a hostage.

ANDREW: I think I have stage-fright.

JAMES: Thirty seconds.

ANDREW: What do you do for stage-fright?

JAMES: I repeat a short quote from a great man.

ANDREW: What is it?

JAMES: You've only got about twenty seconds.

SPENCE: Two minutes K.

ANDREW: Tell me.

JAMES: 'Until I get the same rights my fathers had, I will stand in Jesus' place, convicted as the false prophet, as fire burns and the children starve and the land dies along with the air. I am not broken. I am not beaten. I am my own government.'

ANDREW: Who said that?

JAMES: My favorite hippie:

SPENCE: Ninety seconds.

JAMES: Charlie Manson.

World News Tonight music swells.

ANDREW: Good Evening. My name is Andrew Polackowski, and this is World News Tonight. Some startling developments following the tragic events of yesterday, including new casualty reports and remarkable footage from the front line. But first, we pay tribute to another fallen soldier, VON anchor and network news veteran James Mann who announced his retirement late last night. Mr. Mann's dynamic on-air presence and unquestioned journalist integrity earned him the title 'America's Occasionally Disturbing Bedtime Story', a moniker indicating respect and affection for his pull-no-punches, take-no-prisoners approach to hard news. As his permanent temporary replacement, my goal is simple: Uphold the gold standard defined by this television legend, my friend James Mann, a day-to-day commitment to substantive, fair, and accurate news reporting.

Pause.

And in other news, SAL News Anchor Katherine Mann is a whore.

ANDREW produces an enormous photograph of K engaged in sexual activity. K MANN sucks in a deep breath and screams in shock. Perhaps JAMES does the same.

ANDREW: Verified by two independent sources as un-doctored photographic evidence of total hedonistic sexual debauchery, our network received these photos anonymously in the mail.

SPENCE: You're on in thirty seconds K!

K: What happened? Where did he get those photos? Where did those photos come from? Am I dreaming? Is this a fucking nightmare?

ANDREW: We'll be back after these words.

K: (*Grabbing SPENCE.*) Where did he get those photos?

SPENCE lets dozens of similar photos fall out of his hands onto the ground.

SPENCE: Oh, I have no idea!

K: YOU????

SPENCE: What? These aren't news worthy? Isn't it my journalistic responsibility to alert the media?

K: (*Grabs SPENCE by the throat and slams his head onto the desk, holding it there with hands.*) You think I'm scared of you you little weasel? (*Looking at the audience.*) Go ahead, turn my camera on, I'm ready to go. Turn it on. When I'm done with you you'll be interning for NO PAY. You'll be licking twat for pennies! You'll be sucking ass for dollars! You'll be knocking boots with flip-flops.

K's Nightly News Broadcast music swells. SPENCE is still pinned to the desk by K, trying not to be noticed.

Okay, I'm on? Yes? Good evening ladies and gentlemen. I'm K Mann. New developments in the aftermath of the tragic events of 24-hours ago, but first: No doubt you've just seen photographs of me displayed on national television. These are private photos of private moments, ripped from their intimate context and revealed, no doubt, to tarnish my reputation. This is a desperate, obscene act of sabotage, perpetrated by adolescent hucksters and JEALOUS (*Banging SPENCE'S head for emphasis.*), sniveling middlemen with all the warmth of an extinguished effigy. I am confident, VERY CONFIDENT, that the American people will not be fooled by this calculated insult to their intelligence. I am confident that the viewing public, and my employer the SAL New Organization, will neither judge *nor punish* me for taking pleasure in the geometry of my temporary flesh. What?

K presses her ear-piece. She is receiving a message from the control room.

Oh, I'm fired? WELL FUCK YOU. (*She tosses SPENCE aside.*) I QUIT!

Blackout.

18

ANDREW and SPENCE are now seated side-by-side at JAMES' desk.

SPENCE: ....a bomb which left three dead and 24 wounded. Three radical organization have since claimed responsibility for Tuesday's attack.

ANDREW: A gray-haired Charlie Manson was denied parole today for the eleventh time after telling prison officials he's 'just too busy to be free'. Mr. Manson will be up for parole again in 2006.

SPENCE: And that just about does it for us. Make sure you tune at ten for Nighttalk. Until then I'm Spencer Davis.

ANDREW: And I'm Andrew Polackowski, and this has been World News Tonight, America's Most Popular National News Broadcast.

Blackout.

19

K is seated at her desk. JAMES is standing near her.

K: And the Waitsfield County School Board has reported a budget surplus in excess of ten dollars for the third year in a row. This is good news for the school district, which has been plagued with a wide-range of problems lately, including a flat-tire on the bus and several playground fights. Now let's turn to James with the weather, Dad?

JAMES: Blow, winds, crack your cheeks. Rage, blow,
You cataracts and hurricanes, spout
'Til you have drenched our steeples, drowned the cocks,
You sulph'rous and thought-executing fires,
Vaunt-couriers to oak-cleaving thunderbolts,
Singe my white head!

K: Now, are we going to see any part of that storm here in Waitsfield County?

JAMES: Not likely Katherine.

K: Thanks Dad.

JAMES: My pleasure.

K: And that just about does it for us. Before we go tonight, I'd like to take a moment to thank the kind people of Durham, and the surrounding Waitsfield County. You have welcomed us into your small community with open arms, and my father and I thank you. Though our big city ways and dog-eared past may have come as a shock to your delicate system, you have since recovered, and shown us your smile. From Adelphia Cable Station 36 to all you in Durham, and the surrounding Waitsfield County, I'm K Mann.

JAMES: And I'm James Mann.

K / JAMES: Good night.

End

PUGILIST SPECIALIST

Characters

LT. EMMA STEIN
LT. STUDDARD
LT. TRAVIS FREUD
COL. JOHNS

Notes on production

In *Pugilist Specialist* four marines are assigned the task of
eliminating a Middle-Eastern leader. Throughout the
preparation, training, and execution of the plan their
conversations are recorded. The locations suggested by the
dialogue are various rooms in a barracks, a messhall, an
airplane, a desert, and a palace.

This play was originally produced for the stage by The Riot Group. It opened at the Pleasance Theatre, Edinburgh, on August 1, 2003 with the following cast:

LT. EMMA STEIN, Stephanie Viola

LT. STUDDARD, Drew Friedman

LT. TRAVIS FREUD, Adriano Shaplin

COL. JOHNS, Paul Schnabel

Directed by The Riot Group

Produced by Louise J. Chantal

This production received the Fringe First Award, the First of the Firsts Award and the Herald Angel Award. The Riot Group were nominated for a Stage Award for Best Ensemble.

Pugilist Specialist

1

LT. EMMA STEIN sits alone in a military briefing room. A microphone is suspended from the ceiling.

LT. STEIN: Loneliness.
　　Mother of grief.
　　I'm early.
　　I am an unwilling preface.
　　That's me.
　　They make promises.
　　Clean breaks. Smash and grab.
　　Quick in-and-out.
　　I know they expect an audience, otherwise my sex would
　　exclude me.
　　They never invite the girls in uniform and forget the
　　cameras.
　　I polish my teeth more often than my boots,
　　unfortunately.
　　I've been instructed to embrace my role as military
　　spokes model.
　　Never mind my expertise, that is more judiciously
　　employed.
　　Meaning rarely.
　　But here I am. Early.
　　This prevents the boys from rehearsing limericks or
　　carving their fantastic gynecological reliefs in the
　　tabletops.
　　Male gossip stinks like napalm in a room,
　　arrive last and you'll see how it makes your eyes water.
　　Punctuality is my feminism. (*Pause.*)
　　Five minutes to go. (*Pause.*)
　　What's your story?
　　Were you an athlete in school?
　　A lesbian?

Was your poor redneck father buried with his boots on?
That's okay. Let the boys think whatever.
I believe in origins.
There are worse things than stories. Worse indignities
than explanation.
Secrets are my armor.
Silence is my camouflage.
Victory forgives dishonesty.
We won't call it a preface. We'll call it a prayer.
Loneliness, grief, discipline.
Spectacles, testicles, wallet, watch.
Decode that.

2

LT. STUDDARD enters the room.

LT. STEIN: Lieutenant Studdard.

LT. STUDDARD: Lieutenant Stein.

LT. STEIN: Long time no see.

LT. STUDDARD: Mm hm.

Pause.

LT. STEIN: Any ideas on this one?

LT. STUDDARD: Mm.

LT. STEIN: No?

LT. STUDDARD: Sure. Some.

LT. STEIN: I wasn't briefed.

LT. STUDDARD: This is the briefing.

LT. STEIN: I know. Just that there was no overview.

Pause.

In my orders.

LT. STUDDARD: Me neither.

Pause.

Feel better?

LT. STEIN: Yes, thank you Lieutenant.

LT. STUDDARD: Mm.

Pause.

LT. STEIN: I made a point of getting here early.

Pause.

Did you become a specialist?

LT. STUDDARD: Communications. Mostly data retrieval.

LT. STEIN: I went into explosives.

LT. STUDDARD: I know Lieutenant Stein.

LT. STEIN: Okay.

Pause.

How did you know?

LT. STUDDARD: You carry a high profile Lieutenant.

LT. STEIN: Right.

LT. STUDDARD: Multiplied by your sex.

LT. STEIN: There's that.

LT. STUDDARD: Sore thumb.

LT. STEIN: Scarlet letter.

LT. STUDDARD: One of those.

LT. STEIN: Yeah.

Pause.

I assume you read about the trouble at Fort Bragg.

LT. STUDDARD: Hm.

LT. STEIN: Not *my* trouble. *The* trouble. I don't think of it as *my* trouble.

LT. STUDDARD: That thing with *The Times* was you?

LT. STEIN: I assumed that was common knowledge.

LT. STUDDARD: I don't think it is.

LT. STEIN: That's good to know.

LT. STUDDARD: Either way. I didn't draw any conclusions.

LT. STEIN: Neither did the disciplinary committee.

LT. STUDDARD: Looks like you came out alright.

LT. FREUD enters.

LT. FREUD: Well well well. Lieutenant Stein.

LT. STEIN: Lieutenant.

LT. FREUD: Harpo.

LT. STUDDARD: Mm.

LT. FREUD: What's the good word? Are we collecting Intel? Hostage rescue? Hm? Silent insertion? I love silent insertion. So romantic.

LT. STEIN: There hasn't been a pre-briefing.

LT. FREUD: No, of course.

LT. STEIN: Of course?

LT. FREUD: I didn't receive one.

LT. STUDDARD: Of course.

LT. FREUD: What do you know Harpo?

LT. STUDDARD: Very little Lieutenant Freud.

LT. FREUD: Come on Harpo. How long have we been friends? Every time I see you it's like we're starting over.

LT. STUDDARD: Hm.

LT. FREUD: (*To STEIN.*) We go way back. And you: I know you.

LT. STEIN: We've never met Lieutenant.

LT. FREUD: You sure? I feel like I know you.

LT. STEIN: I don't think so.

LT. FREUD: Didn't you convince me to join the Marines?

LT. STEIN: We haven't met.

LT. FREUD: We haven't?

LT. STUDDARD: Okay Travis.

LT. FREUD: Let me see if I can remember: 'The Marines, historically, have been leaders in racial and gender integration. Our project is righteous, the playing field is level, and the time...is now.'

LT. STEIN: Why were you watching a minority recruitment tape?

LT. STUDDARD: What's this?

LT. STEIN: I filmed a recruitment tape four years ago.

LT. STUDDARD: For minorities?

LT. FREUD: I'm one-fifth Portuguese.

LT. STEIN: How old are you?

LT. FREUD: That tape really worked. Little thing in tight jungle fatigues –

LT. STEIN: That's lovely. Thank you. Nice to meet you.

LT. STUDDARD: That's enough.

LT. FREUD: – And I get to carry a gun? As opposed to college?

LT. STEIN: Classy.

LT. FREUD: That makes you my manifest destiny. If you know what I mean.

LT. STEIN: I know what you mean Lieutenant.

LT. FREUD: Do you?

LT. STEIN: Sure I do. It's the sad reality of a volunteer army. A bunch of incentive-dependant videogame junkies with permanent erections take the place of men with heart and soul. Your enlisted class resembles that which is skimmed from the surface of old milk.

LT. FREUD: Charmed I'm sure.

LT. STEIN: You are charming. Trot around the world in heavy vehicles lending your brutality to countries unversed in the Tarzan logic of the old guard. I'm so glad I participated in recruitment.

LT. STUDDARD: I think that's enough.

LT. FREUD: What? Did I beat your high score on 'Ms. Pacman' at Fort Bragg?

LT. STEIN: I don't do the smile and nod thing Freud.

LT. FREUD: Harpo, do you appreciate the significance of this pairing? She's the mother of my military career.

LT. STUDDARD: How old are you?

LT. FREUD: The horizon line of my heroic trajectory in this beloved Corp.

LT. STEIN: Don't let my tits be your substitute horizon Freud. That's what the desert is for.

LT. FREUD: What tits? Who said anything about tits?

LT. STUDDARD: Language. Watch your language.

LT. FREUD: No, my mistake. I should trust the bathroom walls for my inside information. Most soldiers doubt you're human. A cyborg. An immaculate conception.

LT. STEIN: I heard test tube baby.

LT. FREUD: Same fucking thing.

LT. STUDDARD: Language.

LT. FREUD: Oh sorry Harpo. I don't possess your stoicism. Teach me.

LT. STUDDARD: For the tapes.

LT. STEIN: What tapes?

LT. STUDDARD: (*Indicating the microphone above them.*) We're live.

LT. FREUD: Live to where?

LT. STUDDARD: Don't know. I wired at 0700.

LT. STEIN: You were here first?

LT. FREUD: Why are they taping us?

LT. STEIN: I'm not sure I'm comfortable with this.

LT. FREUD: Unless, maybe for an audio manual. Maybe this is a non-standard op.

LT. STEIN: No.

LT. FREUD: It stands to reason.

LT. STEIN: This is a briefing for a *mission,* correct?

LT. STUDDARD: Yes.

LT. FREUD: Who cares anyway? I've got nothing to hide.

LT. STUDDARD: Victory forgives dishonesty.

LT. STEIN: Well the Colonel isn't here and I'm not comfortable with surveillance.

LT. FREUD: You aren't comfortable?

Pause.

LT. STEIN: I'm not comfortable with anything supplemental and unnecessary.

LT. FREUD: The cover of *The New York Times* – that's no problem – but this.

LT. STUDDARD: Travis.

LT. FREUD: What, isn't it common knowledge? Her star-studded debut as an unnamed source?

LT. STEIN: You can't make me blush Lieutenant.

LT. FREUD: Marine're full of spies. At least Harpo gets paid to tattle.

LT. STUDDARD: I do data retrieval.

LT. STEIN: Behave yourself and you've got nothing to worry about.

LT. FREUD: Turn around is fair play.

LT. STEIN: If it degrades the quality of our performance: I'm not comfortable with it.

LT. FREUD: Anxiety is good for your performance.

LT. STEIN: My performance record doesn't need any improvement.

LT. FREUD: Performance without anxiety is like a day without sunshine.

LT. STEIN: (*To STUDDARD.*) Lieutenant, is this going to be a cowboy mission? I don't do cowboy missions.

LT. FREUD: That's my favorite kind of mission.

LT. STEIN: That's something I might have predicted.

LT. FREUD: The problem is: Are there enough healthy Indians?

LT. STEIN: Studdard?

LT. STUDDARD: I don't think so. I think this is low profile.

LT. STEIN: With microphones?

LT. FREUD: How ironic. The marine's shining star prefers the cover of night. A woman after my own heart.

LT. STEIN: I like standard, well-organized, government-sanctioned murders. I'm not a goddam cold-war spy.

LT. FREUD: Marines don't murder. They *shape* the enemy.

LT. STEIN: He's a starving artist.

LT. STUDDARD: Makes sense.

LT. STEIN: What?

LT. STUDDARD: (*Jerking his head toward LT. FREUD.*) Sniper.

LT. STEIN: (*To LT. FREUD.*) You're a sniper?

LT. FREUD: I prefer hopeless romantic.

LT. STUDDARD: This must be a minor target mission.

LT. STEIN: Single building or complex?

LT. STUDDARD: I don't know, that's your thing. I'm guessing three to five targets.

LT. FREUD: You know: There is a great deal of mythology surrounding my role, but precious little respect.

LT. STEIN: Did you receive equipment specs?

LT. STUDDARD: Hm.

Short pause.

LT. STEIN: And?

LT. STUDDARD: Four voice-activated open-channel mics. Four twelve-hour battery packs. A mess of jamming equipment and four PBBs.

LT. STEIN: What is that? Protective Body what?

LT. STUDDARD: Personal Black Box.

LT. FREUD: Oh I love those. You can compose your own breathless eulogy.

LT. STEIN: I didn't receive any equipment specs.

LT. FREUD: 'Tell my girlfriend she's pregnant.'

LT. STEIN: Lieutenant Freud?

LT. FREUD: Yeah?

LT. STEIN: Did you receive equipment specs?

LT. FREUD: I brought my gun. But I always bring my gun.

LT. STEIN: I don't do minor target missions and I don't do black ops.

LT. FREUD: What 'don't'? Meaning what?

LT. STEIN: I'm not qualified for para-military ops.

LT. FREUD: What are you qualified for?

LT. STEIN: I do pre-demo. Foundation corruption. Structural contamination. I've done some remote ambush detonation.

LT. STUDDARD: I thought you did the palace banquet in '94?

Pause.

LT. FREUD: *You* did the palace banquet?

LT. STEIN: I *planned* and *supervised* the palace banquet.

LT. STUDDARD: Did you design the instruments?

LT. STEIN: I built and designed the instruments but I was a half-mile away supervising detonation with a commando unit. I never entered the target site.

LT. FREUD: Did you carry?

LT. STEIN: I'm a marine Lieutenant. I carry a fucking gun.

LT. STUDDARD: Language.

LT. FREUD: Listen to you. I'm jealous of the attention you give that microphone.

LT. STEIN: And how do you know about the palace banquet? That was a black-op.

LT. FREUD: Exactly.

LT. STEIN: My *only* black-op.

LT. STUDDARD: Makes sense.

LT. FREUD: Every new day in the uniform is a rash of favors and exemptions for you princess.

LT. STEIN: I doubt very much you'd trade places with me.

LT. FREUD: I would. If only to assume responsibility for that dirty deed. Truly brilliant.

LT. STUDDARD: I've seen the satellite photos from that.

LT. FREUD: Exploding soup bowls. Spoon shrapnel. Flammable tablecloth. And then she dropped the fucking roof on them.

LT. STUDDARD: I remember.

LT. FREUD: It was a whimsical attack. The first truly whimsical remote assassination.

LT. STUDDARD: What flavor soup?

LT. STEIN: I didn't cater the fucking –

Pause.

Crab.

LT. STUDDARD: How many?

LT. FREUD: It was twelve.

LT. STEIN: Thirteen. One target. Six sons. Six daughters.

LT. STUDDARD: They were collateral?

LT. STEIN: No, they were consistent obstructions.

LT. FREUD: See? Black-ops aren't so bad.

LT. STEIN: It's unsportsmanlike. It leaves a bad taste in my mouth.

LT. FREUD: Nahhhhh. Blacks-ops are like blind dates. The bigger the risk the brighter the fireworks.

LT. STUDDARD: Unless the target is unworthy.

LT. FREUD: True Harpo. If she's a dog you just close your eyes and think of Hitler.

LT. STEIN: I'll thank you not to use generic feminine pronouns Lieutenant Freud. We're co-ed today.

LT. FREUD: What if the target is a woman?

LT. STUDDARD: It won't be.

LT. FREUD: Okay. You know something we don't Harpo?

LT. STUDDARD: I can only imagine.

LT. STEIN: I believe the Colonel is late.

LT. FREUD: Every target has a feminine side – present company excluded.

LT. STEIN: Watch yourself Lieutenant.

LT. FREUD: Now I should watch myself? Why don't you get with my program Lieutenant? What are you, FTA?

LT. STEIN: I graduated top of my class Lieutenant. I have no Failure To Adapt. I very much doubt recruit training was more difficult for me than for you. You're the cocky, undisciplined lout.

LT. STUDDARD: Hm.

LT. FREUD: Kiss my grits.

LT. STEIN: Let me make something very clear Lieutenant. I'm not sitting in this room as a party favor nor will I knowingly participate in the degradation of my rank. I'm perfectly willing to spar a bit but I won't tolerate anything that smells like disrespect.

LT. FREUD: Pardon me Lieutenant. I'll make a more genuine effort to conceal my odor.

LT. STEIN: That's all I ask Freud.

LT. FREUD: Thank you Lieutenant.

LT. STEIN: Thank *you* Lieutenant.

COL. JOHNS enters. All three stand at attention.

COL. JOHNS: Okay. At ease Marines.

They sit.

Please take a seat. I'm glad to see you've chosen to arrive early. This briefing will last approximately thirteen minutes during which time you will be rewarded with all knowledge relevant to this mission. I also hope we can learn a bit about each other as we will be working together intimately over the next seventy-two hours.

Pause.

Everyone here? Lieutenant Studdard?

LT. STUDDARD: I wouldn't know sir.

COL. JOHNS: Of course. Sure. You're all here. To Begin: Imprecision. Folly. Sacrifice. (*LT. FREUD coughs.*) Question? No. Okay. Imprecision. Folly. Sacrifice. These are the contagions which are bound to infect any mission executed without proper planning, indoctrination, and passion. My experience tells me these pitfalls widen when a mission bears the extra burden of secrecy. Unfortunately, without secrecy, there would be no clear path to victory, and there we are. Questions? Alright. You'll be assassinating 'Big 'Stach', hereby referred to from this moment until his timely demise as 'The Bearded Lady'. Questions?

Pause.

Any questions?

LT. STEIN: Sir, with all due respect, three Marine battalions and the third infantry spent three months trying to locate –

COL. JOHNS: 'The Bearded Lady.'

LT. STEIN: 'The Bearded Lady.' I'm certain the quality of intel could not be strong enough to deploy a small unit....

COL. JOHNS: The intel is waterproof.

LT. FREUD: Sir, Lieutenant Travis Freud, Fort Poke: Sir, though your proposition intrigues me I would like to pose a question.

COL. JOHNS: Go ahead Lieutenant.

LT. FREUD: It is my understanding that 'Big – '

COL. JOHNS: 'The Bearded Lady.'

LT. FREUD: 'The Bearded Lady' suffers from a range of psychological disorders exasperated by his decadent isolation and extreme wealth. Delusions, paranoia, impotence −

COL. JOHNS: Yes Lieutenant. What is your question?

Pause.

LT. FREUD: Well, I suppose it wasn't so much a question as a comment sir.

COL. JOHNS: Thank you for that Lieutenant. Lieutenant Studdard?

LT. STUDDARD: Fine sir. Only I'm unclear as to my role.

COL. JOHNS: 'Every marine a rifleman', Lieutenant.

LT. STUDDARD: I understand sir.

COL. JOHNS: Primarily you'll be responsible for recording and editing and hour-by-hour audio document detailing the mission. This will be used primarily as a training tool for black-op procedure and, in the event that this document is misinterpreted, or becomes the subject of misinterpretation, you will be expected to toilet this particular document. Alternately, if our actions are celebrated, you will prepare excerpts for distribution.

LT. STUDDARD: I doubt anything will have to be destroyed Colonel.

COL. JOHNS: Not sure I understand you there Lieutenant.

LT. STUDDARD: The least common response to my work is misinterpretation.

COL. JOHNS: Sure thing. Victory forgives dishonesty. Any further questions before we adjourn for the day?

LT. STEIN: Yes sir. How are we going to do it?

COL. JOHNS: Okay sure. Sure thing. We can do that now. I suppose. Sure. Mission plan: You have ten hours special equipment / recon training, a portion of which will require you to familiarize the team with your specialty. A sixteen-hour flight to the desert, and approximately twelve hours to complete your mission, eight of which will be occupied with undercover travel. Our intel is our primary advantage – that and a secure contact with a native rebel unit, which will provide access to the mansion.

LT. STEIN: The mansion?

COL. JOHNS: Yes. With any luck the target will be between silk sheets at the time of intrusion.

LT. STUDDARD: What about doubles?

COL. JOHNS: Decoy and double identification will be part of your recon training, though I've also authorized the elimination of any doubles or look-a-likes.

LT. FREUD: Sir, every man in the country is a look-a-like.

COL. JOHNS: Point taken Lieutenant. Point taken.

Pause.

This is in many ways a standard op. Lieutenant Freud will eliminate perimeter guards –

LT. FREUD: How many perimeter guards?

COL. JOHNS: – Lieutenant Studdard will disable enemy communication systems. Lieutenant Stein, you'll be blowing the door and rigging the place for a forensic wipeout. During this time Studdard and Freud will eliminate the target.

LT. STEIN: Who is functioning as unit commander?

COL. JOHNS: I will be your unit leader Lieutenant Stein, following this briefing I'll be entering special training alongside all of you. Any questions?

LT. FREUD: With all due respect Colonel, wouldn't your wisdom and considerable military experience be better utilized from a secure location?

COL. JOHNS: A secure location? Perhaps a chair with rockers or wheels Lieutenant? I am fifty-one years old and I have very low cholesterol. Does that quiet your concern?

LT. FREUD: Sir —

COL. JOHNS: Let that quiet your concern.

LT. STEIN: Sir?

COL. JOHNS: Yes Lieutenant Stein?

LT. STEIN: Are we to expect any international or domestic backlash against a clandestine political assassination?

COL. JOHNS: I'm sure there will be some.

LT. STEIN: Exactly how big of a backlash, in your estimation?

COL. JOHNS: How big? Well, how long is a piece of string?

Pause.

LT. STEIN: Colonel, sarcasm isn't necessary.

COL. JOHNS: No really: How long is a piece of string?

Pause.

LT. STEIN: I simply asked for your estimation.

LT. FREUD: Nine inches. That's my guess.

COL. JOHN: Thank you Lieutenant Freud. Does that answer your question Lieutenant?

LT. STEIN: Colonel do we have a choice?

COL. JOHNS: A choice Lieutenant?

LT. STEIN: Do we possess the option to decline this mission?

COL. JOHNS: I consider your commitment to this mission a choice Lieutenant. And I believe you've made the right choice.

LT. STEIN: That is not a choice I've made.

LT. STUDDARD: Emma...

COL. JOHNS: I think you should tread lightly Lieutenant.

LT. STEIN: Permission to speak freely Colonel?

COL. JOHNS: I'll grant you permission to articulate your confusion about the definition of 'choice'.

LT. STEIN: I'm not confused as to the definition sir. I'm unclear as to the conditions which shape that choice.

Pause.

COL. JOHNS: Speak freely Lieutenant. What would make you happy?

LT. STEIN: Sir: Happy will it be if our choice should be directed by a judicious estimate of our true interests, unperplexed and unbiased by considerations not connected with the public good.

Pause.

LT. FREUD: Colonel, this might be a good time to let you know that Lieutenant Stein does not speak for me. Lieutenant Stein's career is inoculated against the consequences of dissent. Mine, like many, is nourished by obedience.

COL. JOHNS: Or something resembling obedience?

LT. FREUD: Whatever you like, Colonel.

COL. JOHNS: And how do you feel Lieutenant Freud?

LT. FREUD: Feel?

COL. JOHNS: Yes Lieutenant.

LT. FREUD: Permission to speak freely?

COL. JOHNS: Yes yes, go ahead.

LT. FREUD: Sir, our true interests are for you to know and me to fire at the target. I'd rather not share a pillow with the public good.

COL. JOHNS: Studdard? Would you like to make a formal statement regarding your involvement in this mission?

LT. STUDDARD: I stand not with the advocates of disunion.

COL. JOHNS: Who is your advocate?

LT. STUDDARD: The dead will speak for me sir. I remain neutral.

COL. JOHNS: A historian never confesses his bias.

LT. STUDDARD: A historian has no bias.

COL. JOHNS: Good boy. As to your happiness Lieutenant Stein: Happiness is a thing more ardently to be wished than seriously to be expected. Regarding your choice: Our passions will color this thankless affair, lending glory to an otherwise tawdry event. We will be the bigger men, architects of liberty. We will sacrifice ourselves, but first and foremost, we will sacrifice the lives of our enemies, and school them in the manners and etiquette of death. We will seduce their bodies, steal their breath, bury them with heads pointing toward Mecca, and collect memories of their forgotten cause. (*To STUDDARD.*) That'll be your job. As their race is the chosen body of our righteous intervention, we will honor their unfortunate wishes and make every effort to preserve the dignity of their ravished corpses. Each corpse will index our cause, and document the unfolding destiny of this magnificent empire.

Pause.

And if there is nothing else I'd like to direct you to the mess hall for hot dogs and salad. Dismissed. Lieutenant Stein, my office please.

Pause.

COL. JOHNS exits.

LT. FREUD: You'll thank me later.

LT. STEIN: Yeah, with a brick.

LT. FREUD: Promises promises.

LT. STUDDARD: Do you know where the mess hall is Emma?

LT. STEIN: I'll find it.

3

LT. FREUD: You're eating salad.

LT. STUDDARD: I don't eat hot dogs.

LT. FREUD: Why not?

LT. STUDDARD: It's garbage civilian food.

LT. FREUD: Don't be a hard-ass Harpo.

LT. STUDDARD: It gives you the runs.

LT. FREUD: 'Garbage Civilian Food'. You're such a leatherneck.

LT. STUDDARD: Lieutenant Freud, you're so unconventional.

LT. FREUD: Okay. You wanna race? First one to eat five hot-dogs.

LT. STUDDARD: No thanks.

LT. FREUD: No buns. Just the dogs. Make it ten. But you can't drink anything in between.

LT. STUDDARD: I'd be afraid to win.

LT. FREUD: You're afraid to win?

LT. STUDDARD: Sure.

LT. FREUD: A marine should never be afraid to win.

LT. STUDDARD: We're talking about hot dogs, right?

LT. FREUD: Okay, fifteen hot dogs. No mustard.

LT. STUDDARD: You have a very volatile personality.

LT. FREUD: You don't fool me Studdard. Race me with hot dogs. You know you want to.

LT. STUDDARD: Hm.

LT. FREUD: I eat unconscious desires for breakfast.

LT. STUDDARD: Uh huh.

LT. FREUD: What's your excuse Studdard? Did someone touch you a long time ago?

LT. STUDDARD: If at first you don't succeed, redefine success.

LT. FREUD: Okay Yoda. I call you coward.

LT. STUDDARD: Then call me.

LT. FREUD: Coward. What kind of marine would refuse a plate of fine pork hot dogs? This is life reconstituted into a delicious and compact form. This hot dog will fit in your throat and slide out your ass. It is the distillation of some swine's hopes and dreams, the reordered flesh of a once noisy creature. Someone took the raw material of life and transformed it into something meaningful, and beautiful and delicious. And it is your responsibility to consume this hot dog and transform it into energy;

energy which will assist you in the seduction and evaporation of our enemies. There is no such thing as a vegetarian killer Harpo. This is also true of artists like myself. An artist breeds, bleeds, and consumes the best part of this world. Race me with hot dogs. I promise: You'll shit a sculpture too radiant for words, sign the canvas and have a glass of wine.

Pause.

LT. STUDDARD: Do you want your apple pie?

LT. FREUD: Yes.

LT. STUDDARD: Okay. First one to finish fifteen gets the other's dessert: One...

4

COL. JOHNS: Alright Lieutenant. Maybe I don't look like a pacifist to you. Maybe I'm just one more gray crew cut in a long line of faceless father figures. Maybe I'm some pitiless jarhead with no sense of direction, so I took a job that lets me carry a compass. Maybe I'm just a babysitter to you, and you're just waiting for mom and dad to come home. But I think you misjudge me Lieutenant. I think I can make you comfortable here. I can help you out of that dress and into something more comfortable. I want to negotiate a treaty with that body Lieutenant, and do business with your mind.

LT. STEIN: Sir, I don't waste time dodging exploitation. You want me in front of cameras with medals on my chest? I'll be there. My mind, and my ability, speaks for itself. Anything else you want me to say: I'll say it.

COL. JOHNS: You are everything we need and everything we don't. A PR dream wrapped in a logistical nightmare. A pretty face – evidence of the glory of American democracy, equality, and integration – or someone's daughter in a body bag, crippling the resolve of our loyal hawks.

LT. STEIN: What do you want from me Colonel?

COL. JOHNS: Apart from your cooperation I don't want anything from you Lieutenant. You aren't here to be the celebrity grunt. I wanted a lonely-hearts club. Bachelors and childless women. Bearers of the scarlet letter of loneliness. We want to be sure our passions don't dilute our focus.

LT. STEIN: Is that all Colonel?

COL. JOHNS: I'll let you be the soldier you want to be Lieutenant. Good with bombs. Anonymous. Just give me some loyalty. Keep this mission off the cover of *The New York Times.*

LT. STEIN: You shouldn't worry about my loyalty to the cause Colonel. Success is my feminism, unrestricted by any crisis of conscience.

COL. JOHNS: I thought punctuality was your feminism?

LT. STEIN: (*Looks up at microphone.*) I was here on time wasn't I?

5

LT. FREUD: Hey Stein.

LT. STEIN: Lieutenant.

LT. FREUD: Go ahead and tell her Harpo.

LT. STEIN: Tell me what?

LT. FREUD: I've robbed Lieutenant Studdard of his fragile masculinity.

LT. STEIN: Super.

LT. FREUD: Seriously, when does life get hard? I'm ready to jump out and scare life. Recent victories have stiffened by resolve.

LT. STEIN: Did you see cheeseburgers up there, or just hamburgers?

LT. FREUD: If the marines don't kill me I'll have to journey to the center of the earth and ingest its creamy vanilla filling.

LT. STEIN: I don't think we're in good hands with the Colonel.

LT. STUDDARD: What makes you say that?

LT. STEIN: I think he's a feminist.

LT. STUDDARD: I thought he was a nihilist?

LT. FREUD: Feminist, nihilist: Same fucking thing.

LT. STEIN: Pass the carrots.

LT. STUDDARD: What did he want to talk about?

LT. STEIN: He's one of those.

LT. STUDDARD: Which?

LT. STEIN: Advocates of Sensitive Leadership.

LT. FREUD: Was he gentle?

LT. STEIN: I think he wants to be my friend.

LT. FREUD: God forbid.

LT. STUDDARD: He's from the new school.

LT. FREUD: A little old for the new school isn't he?

LT. STEIN: Probably just a Failure To Adapt. All the older brass have daddy issues.

LT. FREUD: Or political aspirations.

LT. STEIN: Same thing.

LT. FREUD: She gets it.

LT. STUDDARD: What did he actually say?

LT. STEIN: He's an acid casualty. Probably never read the Constitution. He thinks war is his personal masturbation fantasy.

LT. FREUD: Whatever floats your boat.

LT. STEIN: Whatever floats his boat.

LT. STUDDARD: He seemed fine when I talked to him this morning.

Pause.

LT. STEIN: You talked to him this morning?

LT. FREUD: You can talk?

LT. STEIN: Before the briefing?

LT. STUDDARD: I had a pre-briefing this morning.

LT. STEIN: You said you didn't.

LT. STUDDARD: I said there was no overview in my orders.

LT. FREUD: Come on Stein, don't play dumb. Harpo is internal affairs. You can't trust a word he says. He baby-sits that tape.

LT. STEIN: Fine. You had a pre-briefing. You could have told us we were working for John Juan up there.

LT. FREUD: Don.

LT. STEIN: What?

LT. FREUD: Don Juan. Not John Juan. I'm one-fifth Portuguese.

LT. STUDDARD: I didn't see any reason to be concerned.

LT. STEIN: He's creepy.

LT. FREUD: It's a good thing we cut danger out of the war thing, otherwise I'd be worried.

LT. STEIN: I'm not worried. I'm concerned.

LT. FREUD: Let go and let God.

LT. STUDDARD: God has nothing to do with it.

LT. FREUD: How about arm-wrestling? Would you like to arm-wrestle? Recover some dignity?

LT. STUDDARD: You didn't capture my dignity.

LT. FREUD: I didn't?

LT. STUDDARD: You didn't.

LT. FREUD: Well what is this in my stomach? It doesn't feel like a belly full of hot-dogs. It kicks and turns like a frightened dignity covered in soft fur and searching wildly for its father. Not to worry dad: Your dignity will remain imprisoned in my guts until it crawls from my busy birth canal twelve hours from now – at which point I will gently suggest that you reabsorb this brown orphan. Orally.

LT. STEIN: Jesus, my appetite is not the enemy.

LT. STUDDARD: If my dignity is in your guts why don't I just go in and get it.

LT. FREUD: That sounds mildly erotic.

LT. STUDDARD: It was meant to sound violent.

LT. FREUD: It didn't.

LT. STEIN: (*Looking up.*) These tapes aren't being archived, by the way. They're being reviewed daily.

LT. STUDDARD: That's standard protocol.

LT. STEIN: Standard for what?

LT. FREUD: You wanna arm-wrestle Stein? I can't get a rematch from 'He-who-hath-surrendered-his-dignity'.

LT. STUDDARD: I want to clarify that he ate twelve hot dogs faster than me. That's what happened.

LT. FREUD: That's the problem with the official record Harpo, it has no odor.

LT. STUDDARD: I'm losing my patience with you.

LT. FREUD: Your patience and your dignity? This just isn't your day.

LT. STEIN: Stop it please. I give up, okay? You are both hard as nails with nerves of steel. I'm very impressed. Now no more pissing contests. I'm trying to eat.

LT. FREUD: That's a good idea. We'll have a pissing contest. Wait, I'm the only one with a dick. How about a little arm-wrestling?

LT. STEIN: You don't fool me Freud.

LT. FREUD: I don't?

LT. STEIN: I know you just want to hold hands.

LT. FREUD laughs.

LT. STUDDARD: This is going to be a long week.

LT. FREUD: You're quite the little filibuster. Would you like to have nine of my babies?

LT. STEIN: That task would likely require half the energy of tolerating a single conversation with you.

LT. FREUD: Well, that's my new hobby: Watching steam come out of your ears.

LT. STUDDARD: I have to go get ready.

LT. STEIN: Evolve or die. That's all I've got to say.

LT. FREUD: Is that all you have to say?

LT. STEIN: That's it.

LT. FREUD: Well, happy birthday to me.

6

LT. STUDDARD: Satellite microphones.

COL. JOHNS: Oh?

LT. STUDDARD: I developed a new type of satellite microphone. Better range and clarity.

COL. JOHNS: Well, why don't I just bring the satellite microphones and leave you behind?

LT. STUDDARD: I don't know. I assume because of my interpretation skills.

COL. JOHNS: You speak Arabic?

LT. STUDDARD: No.

Pause.

COL. JOHNS: Go ahead Lieutenant Studdard.

LT. STUDDARD: There are ten major encryption protocols used in the region, which correspond to the executive launch codes outlined in 1988. We will be utilizing two simultaneous frequencies which will complement each other and, in all likelihood, fill in for each other in case of regional or weather-related disturbance.

COL. JOHNS: Can you just give us the long-and-short of it?

LT. STUDDARD: Not really Colonel.

COL. JOHNS: Just give us the essence, the spirit of it.

LT. STUDDARD: Sir, in the event of my incapacitation the 'spirit' of our communication frequency isn't going to rise up and take charge.

COL. JOHNS: Well, there are no atheists in the foxhole.

LT. FREUD: What's a foxhole?

LT. STUDDARD: With all due respect sir, atheists make the best historians.

COL. JOHNS: No, deconstructionists make the best historians.

LT. STUDDARD: Sir, I'm not sure that even makes sense.

LT. FREUD: Colonel, can we go?

LT. STEIN: What 'we'? I'm not going anywhere with you.

COL. JOHN: Is this really you Lieutenant? You couldn't possibly be this boring.

Pause.

LT. STUDDARD: Hm.

COL. JOHNS: Make us *feel* why your role is important. Make us *care* that you're alive for God's sake. I like our *target* more than I like you.

LT. STUDDARD: Sir, I thought I was supposed to…

COL. JOHNS: Make us *feel* encryption protocols.

LT. STUDDARD: Sir, there is no feeling in what I do. I establish the lines of communication. I record. I translate. I archive. I'm either calling it in or writing it down. I'm not tongue-kissing anyone.

COL. JOHNS: Can you believe this Lieutenant Stein?

LT. STEIN: Sure, I've known Studdard a long time.

COL. JOHNS: Freud?

LT. FREUD: I'm beside myself.

COL. JOHNS: What is history Studdard? Is it a terribly good excuse to bump heads? Is it the best argument against hope?

LT. STEIN: It is a terribly good excuse to bump...

COL. JOHNS: It's a bedtime story.

Pause.

LT. STUDDARD: Should I continue or...

COL. JOHNS: It's the most dangerous narcotic on the market. You'd think advances in high-speed media technology would help people kick the habit of history, but we've got stubborn, dusty addicts like you producing and distributing hot shots all over the place.

LT. STUDDARD: Sir, every conflict has a context.

COL. JOHNS: What's so special or so comforting about a back-story?

LT. STUDDARD: Colonel I'm proud to be part of the most sensitive fact-checking organization in the world.

LT. FREUD: He's very sensitive.

COL. JOHNS: Well are you a stenographer or a soldier?

LT. STEIN: Sir, can I say something?

COL. JOHNS: Go ahead Lieutenant.

LT. STEIN: I think Lieutenant Studdard is trying to say that those who don't know history are doomed...

COL. JOHNS: Let me be doomed. What's the big deal with being 'doomed to repeat'? I'm alive aren't I? I woke up this morning. I wouldn't mind repeating that.

LT. STEIN: I just don't think it's necessary...

COL. JOHNS: As long as I'm alive please let me be doomed to repeat. I'd rather be alive and ignorant than dead and 'sensitive to the facts'. We've got a nation of teenage poets cultivating a rich crop of sensitivity. Where do I get my warriors?

LT. STUDDARD: Sir, someone has to...

COL. JOHNS: We'll need a government program to breed tough litters of clueless enforcers, raised in video arcades, isolated from all this poisonous 'history'.

LT. STUDDARD: Colonel I'm...

COL. JOHNS: I think this mission will be good for you Lieutenant... Help you use your left-brain.

LT. STUDDARD: You mean my right-brain?

COL. JOHNS: One of those.

Pause.

LT. STUDDARD: Permission to speak freely Colonel?

COL. JOHNS: Only if you're planning to account for this little fetish for evidence. And only if you're planning to explain how this kinky little ritual wins wars.

LT. STUDDARD: Sir, I believe all rhetorical questions are accusations.

COL. JOHNS: Is that it?

LT. STUDDARD: Sir, any absence of passion is a by-product of my pitiless career. I'm a baby-sitter. I take care of the words when they lose their bodies. That's my job. I don't need a heart. I've got reels of incriminating evidence. I handle spools of careless conversation. I preside over a kingdom of sound bites and transcripts.

Pause.

Would you like to know why I'm quiet? Is that your question? Why I refrain from all your chatter? I know where loose talk goes to die. Loose talk is slow to decompose. I know the generous afterlife of gossip. I know how easy it is to make a memory. There is a reason that peace and quiet are partners. This is why a soldier prefers deafness. Because the blind are condemned to a life of eavesdropping. Have any of you spent a significant amount of time eavesdropping? You'll beg for deafness.

Pause.

I've got enough passion and chatter collecting dust on my shelf, Sir.

Pause.

COL. JOHNS: Okay. That was good. Freud, can you familiarize us with your role later this afternoon?

LT. FREUD: Yeah, that'll be fun.

7

LT. STEIN: That's him.

COL. JOHNS: Freud?

LT. FREUD: I'm saying that's the double.

COL. JOHNS: Studdard?

LT. STUDDARD: The double.

Pause.

COL. JOHNS: That's him.

LT. FREUD: What is wrong with me?

LT. STEIN: Travis, did you get a copy of the identification brochure?

LT. FREUD: Harpo didn't get it right either.

LT. STEIN: Am I the only one who has actually taken the time to study this goddam CENTCOM twelve-step identification brochure?

LT. FREUD: Well I still don't think that's him.

COL. JOHNS: Well, Lieutenant Freud, you just misidentified the primary target. We don't want any missed opportunities.

LT. FREUD: Hey, I guessed it was the double. That doesn't mean I'm not taking the shot.

LT. STEIN: Then what's the point Travis?

LT. FREUD: There is no point. I'm clipping anything with a mustache.

COL. JOHNS: Lieutenant Freud. Let's take this seriously.

LT. FREUD: Oh, I'm serious. You said we're taking out the doubles. Why do we need to spend seven hours learning how to do mole-to-pupil distance ratios?

COL. JOHNS: Why Lieutenant Studdard?

LT. STUDDARD: We have to know where and when we hit 'The Bearded Lady', otherwise we won't know when we're done.

COL. JOHNS: I thought you'd be good at this Lieutenant Freud.

LT. STEIN: I'm not wasting my primary instrument on a body-double Freud.

LT. FREUD: Well, you're scoring ninety per cent so don't worry about it.

COL. JOHNS: Fine. Lieutenant Studdard, what was the source of your miscalculation?

LT. STUDDARD: Well sir, I'd like to point out that I've been going third, so my first instincts are being influenced by Stein and Freud's guesses.

LT. FREUD: Okay, that's my excuse too.

LT. STEIN: What are you, a collie dog? Don't use your instincts Harpo, employ the goddam rational method of analysis outlined in the CENTCOM brochure.

LT. STUDDARD: Emma, I was up all night...

COL. JOHNS: Lieutenant Stein, how did you know this was 'The Bearded Lady'?

LT. STEIN: It was a combination of the mild cauliflower around the ear and the redundant tissue in the cheeks.

LT. STUDDARD: The jowls?

LT. STEIN: That's more than a set of jowls, that's redundant tissue.

COL. JOHNS: I wouldn't rely on that if I were you.

LT. STEIN: I'm scoring ninety per cent.

COL. JOHNS: Okay, put down that goddam brochure. It isn't working.

LT. STUDDARD: Colonel I just didn't have any time to review the brochure in detail...

COL. JOHNS: Forget the brochure. It didn't work for Freud.

LT. STUDDARD: With all due respect sir...

LT. FREUD: Don't say it Harpo.

COL. JOHNS: Try this one.

Pause.

LT. STEIN: That's the double.

LT. STUDDARD: Okay. The double. I'm guessing the double.

COL. JOHNS: Look at the eyes Freud. Do you notice a certain quality?

192

LT. FREUD: Brown.

COL. JOHNS: No. I mean, yes, brown. But do you notice a vaguely seductive quality?

LT. STEIN: What? Is that the target?

COL. JOHNS: Would you like to change your guess?

LT. STEIN: No. That's the double.

COL. JOHNS: Lieutenant Freud?

LT. FREUD: I don't know. The double?

COL. JOHNS: That's the target.

LT. STEIN: That can't be him. The mole placement isn't right.

COL. JOHNS: She's wearing make-up. We can't pin down the location of that beauty mark with any certainty. Look at the eyes.

LT. STEIN: Are you positive Colonel?

COL. JOHNS: Look at the eyes Stein. That's our target. Do you see it? Freud? What do you see?

LT. FREUD: A vaguely seductive quality?

COL. JOHNS: Bedroom eyes.

LT. STEIN: Bedroom eyes?

COL. JOHNS: She's like dove.

LT. FREUD: Yeah. With a mustache.

LT. STEIN: I'm not sure 'bedroom eyes' will register through infrared goggles.

LT. FREUD: I don't know how we're supposed to see anything in these crappy photos anyway. Who took these?

LT. STUDDARD: I took these.

COL. JOHNS: Are you picking up what I'm putting down here Studdard?

LT. STUDDARD: Sir, I'm not even sure what bedroom eyes are.

COL. JOHNS: Bedroom eyes. You know. Like Rudolph Valentino. Or Raul Julia.

Pause.

LT. STEIN: No, it's the frown lines. The frown lines are a dead giveaway.

COL. JOHNS: The eyes don't lie.

LT. STUDDARD: Maybe if I redesign Freud's scope?

LT. FREUD: Sir, why don't you slip between the sheets. That way we can be certain we've eliminated the Arab with the kindest eyes.

COL. JOHNS: I'm disappointed Lieutenant.

LT. FREUD: Colonel I honestly can't tell them apart.

LT. STUDDARD: What if I redesign your scope?

LT. FREUD: I don't use a scope. I use opera glasses.

8

LT. STUDDARD: 'Dear American Heroes, Hello. I am ten. My dad says it's okay to hate the war but we shouldn't hate the soldiers because they are poor high school dropouts from rural areas. Then again, the U.S. Army does possess the largest class of black executives of any major private or government body.' Is that true?

LT. STEIN: I don't know. Is he in private school?

LT. STUDDARD: Read yours.

LT. STEIN: 'Dear Army Man' – Great I get the ten-year-old sexist.

LT. STUDDARD: All ten-year-olds are sexist.

LT. FREUD: Don't these little crumb snatchers know the goddam difference between the Army and the Marines?

LT. STUDDARD: What's the difference Travis?

LT. STEIN: 'I am nine years old. Could you beat up my dad in a fight? My teacher says "Big 'Stache" is like Hitler. This comparison must refer to Hitler's legacy of ethnic and religious genocide, rather than his nationalist grab for global power which would correspond more accurately to the contemporary American policy of...' Is this supposed to boost my morale?

LT. FREUD: Little know-it-all. I'm glad I skipped fourth grade.

LT. STEIN: Blah blah blah 'nation-building' blah blah 'Christian war machine' blah blah 'love Tommy, Burlington Vermont.'

LT. FREUD: 'Christian war machine'?

LT. STUDDARD: Kids say the darndest things.

LT. STEIN: What'd you get?

LT. FREUD: 'Dear Hero, My mom says America is the most immoral, totalitarian force in modern history. But if that is true, how come we have the biggest kitchens in the world?'

LT. STUDDARD: How does he know?

LT. FREUD: She.

LT. STUDDARD: How does she know we have the biggest kitchens in the world?

LT. FREUD: Blah blah 'charred remains of Iraqi babies' yadda yadda 'peace be with you' love, some Asian kid. Why does everyone love babies so much? Every asshole you ever met was a goddam baby!

LT. STUDDARD: I don't want to kill babies.

LT. FREUD: Wars should be fought by babies. They're the most cold-blooded little assholes AND they don't care if they live or die.

LT. STEIN: Stop trying to be shocking. Babies are the reservoirs of human potential.

LT. FREUD: Everyone loves babies all of a sudden! What are you pro-life?

COL. JOHNS: Why are you talking about babies?

LT. STUDDARD: Freud thinks wars should be fought by babies.

COL. JOHNS: Why?

LT. STUDDARD: Because they are cold-blooded and fearless.

COL. JOHNS: Forget it. You need empathy to fight a war. Babies have no empathy.

LT. FREUD: I don't have empathy.

LT. STEIN: Even I don't have empathy.

COL. JOHNS: Trust me, you've got empathy.

LT. FREUD: Not Studdard though. He definitely doesn't have it.

LT. STUDDARD: I couldn't even define it.

LT. FREUD: Well sure! I can't *define* it.

LT. STEIN: You can't define empathy?

LT. FREUD: I'm a sniper, not a playwright. Can *you* define it?

LT. STEIN: Sure: It's a noun meaning 'the ability to understand and share the feelings of another'.

LT. FREUD: Use it in a sentence.

LT. STEIN: Oh shut the fuck up.

COL. JOHNS: 'The sniper empathized with his target, reflecting woefully on the brutal dance of death just prior to pulling the trigger.'

LT. STEIN: Wouldn't the presence of empathy stop him from pulling the trigger?

COL. JOHNS: On the contrary. That's my point.

Pause.

No.

LT. FREUD: I don't want empathy.

LT. STUDDARD: I guess I don't know what I'm missing.

LT. STEIN: You're not missing much. Muscle-memory beats empathy every time.

LT. FREUD: It's like rock-paper-scissors.

COL. JOHNS: But empathy beats intelligence.

LT. STEIN: Muscle memory, intelligence... / Same fuckin' thing.

LT. FREUD: Same fuckin' thing. Great minds. (*Pause.*) Think alike.

LT. STUDDARD: Colonel, should we reseal these letters and forward them to the Navy?

COL. JOHNS: Very funny Harpo, give me the goddam letters.

LT. STEIN: That was good.

LT. FREUD: Funniest thing he's ever said.

LT. STEIN: Fuckin' kids.

LT. FREUD: Who needs 'em.

9

COL. JOHNS: Okay, this the nice part.

LT. STEIN: I hate this.

COL. JOHNS: We've got to leave something nice underneath the tree.

LT. FREUD: If only they had trees.

LT. STUDDARD: Where are we dropping these?

COL. JOHNS: These are the most current standard-issue care packages, which are to be distributed proportional to the number of targets planned or improvised.

LT. STUDDARD: We're playing tooth fairy.

COL. JOHNS: Problem Studdard?

LT. STUDDARD: Not at all.

LT. STEIN: Put them under the pillow.

LT. FREUD: I ain't no fairy.

LT. STEIN: I saw that coming.

COL. JOHNS: We're cutting back on the food bank stuff. Nothing keeps in that heat.

LT. FREUD: I thought Lieutenant Stein was in charge of the 'care packages'.

LT. STEIN: Cluster packages. Thank you.

COL. JOHNS: You'll be the good cop, she'll be the bad cop.

LT. FREUD: I can't be the good cop. I'm playing cupid.

LT. STUDDARD: I'll drop the packages.

COL. JOHNS: Thank you Lieutenant.

LT. STEIN: Is that how we're wrapping them?

COL. JOHNS: The paper is recyclable.

LT. FREUD: You can't trust them to recycle.

LT. STUDDARD: What's inside? Do I have to hold them upright?

LT. FREUD: 'Is that how we're wrapping them?'

LT. STEIN: It's bright orange.

COL. JOHNS: Each package contains: One protein bar. Honey-peanut I think. One miniature white flag. A calculator. And three condoms.

LT. STEIN: They should get candy.

LT. FREUD: No, they need our protein.

LT. STUDDARD: Condoms?

COL. JOHNS: And then we've got these cartoons. Which are instructional.

LT. STUDDARD: What do they need condoms for?

LT. STEIN: Ooo, let me see the cartoons.

LT. FREUD: It's like: 'Immigrate to the U.S., and you might need these.'

LT. STUDDARD: Hm.

LT. FREUD: 'Provided you shave your dirty beard.'

LT. STEIN: Look at this, this is total propaganda.

LT. STUDDARD: Let's not use the word 'propaganda'. (*Looks at microphone.*)

COL. JOHNS: Watch it Stein.

LT. STEIN: Okay, what is 'The Bearded Lady' doing in this picture?

LT. STUDDARD: I think that picture speaks for itself.

LT. FREUD: It's a harmless allegory.

COL. JOHNS: Nothing would be crueler than the truth. Consider our enemies coddled by this propaganda.

LT. STEIN: Do you think because you drew an arrow from 'The Bearded Lady' to a pile of money that his people will rise against him?

LT. FREUD: More importantly, will they know that's a stack of ones?

COL. JOHNS: A strong narrative arch is essential to any military victory. You should know that.

LT. STEIN: This narrative arch has poor character development.

COL. JOHNS: Let me worry about the sentence structure. Studdard will pick the descriptive nouns. Freud will provide colorful adjectives. You worry about the exclamation point at the end.

LT. FREUD: Fuckin' Charlie Rose over here.

LT. STEIN: Why are we dropping this shit? Why are we operating 'under cover of night'? If this operation is such an international blockbuster why are fiddling around with care packages and agit-prop and fucking maps and manifestos and mission statements? What the fuck kind of ethical stand needs to be figured out at a conference table?

LT. FREUD: Ethical what now?

COL. JOHNS: Do you need to get some water Lieutenant Stein?

LT. STEIN: Is it just me? Studdard? Shouldn't the wisdom and logic of any mission be self-evident? I don't want to waste a perfectly good instrument on a half-baked grudge killing that is in constant need of cosmetic tinkering.

LT. STUDDARD: Alright Emma, don't quote Ben Franklin just because you want the nation to admire your fireworks.

LT. STEIN: It has nothing to do with vanity.

LT. STUDDARD: Not every soldier in this unit desires recognition above all things.

LT. FREUD: You're not exactly famous for keeping your finger in the dyke.

COL. JOHNS: You're too self-involved Lieutenant Stein. You need to think about someone else for a change.

LT. STEIN: I seem to be the only one attending to the big picture.

COL. JOHNS: You want a big picture? They either love us or they love to hate us. Either way we're spreading love.

LT. STEIN: It's chaos. Not affection.

COL. JOHNS: You think 'The Bearded Lady' wants to be left alone? More importantly, do you think 'The Bearded Lady' wants to come out on top? We could call him up – Studdard has his phone number – and say 'Hey Bearded Lady, be my leader. Put my wife in a big sock and take away my magazines.' Do you think he'd be happy? In no way. In no way would he be happy. Everyone loves an underdog.

LT. FREUD: If we didn't kick that guy's ass no one would know he existed. He'd never get laid.

LT. STEIN: Aren't you the one that wants to do the laying Cupid?

LT. FREUD: I'm killing two birds with one stone.

COL. JOHNS: That's why they call it the 'little death' Lieutenant, because it's a fine line between orgasm and eternity.

LT. STUDDARD: I thought it was because your heart skipped a beat.

LT. STEIN: That's sneezing.

LT. STUDDARD: What are we talking about?

LT. FREUD: Listen to me Emma, his cock-sucking religion says when I kiss him goodnight he gets to nail sixty-nine virgins or whatever. We're doing him a favor.

LT. STEIN: It says he's 'met' by seventy-two virgins, it doesn't say anything about 'nailing them'.

LT. FREUD: Well what are they going to do, wash his back?

COL. JOHNS: 'Met' by virgins. 'Met' is biblical code for 'screwed'.

LT. STEIN: Biblical code? He doesn't read the bible!

LT. FREUD: What are you? A prisoner of conscience?

COL. JOHNS: 'Koran' is Arabic code for 'Bible'. Right Studdard?

LT. STUDDARD: No.

COL. JOHNS: Look at me? Tell me I don't respect the dignity of our target? I'm dressed up like her goddam ancient Mesopotamian landscape tapestry of indigenous plant life.

LT. FREUD: His underwear is desert-camo.

LT. STEIN: You have no idea do you? I can't be a part of a failed mission. I can't ride shotgun on an aborted black-op. Do you have any idea happens when missions involving women fail? Women lose their pensions.

COL. JOHNS: What do you suggest Lieutenant Stein?

LT. STEIN: I think we should tighten this up a little. At the very least we should double our personnel.

LT. FREUD: Fucking 'personnel'. This isn't Office Depot.

LT. STUDDARD: She means manpower.

LT. FREUD: Whatever.

LT. STEIN: We shouldn't rely on native informants.

COL. JOHNS: We're not planning a wedding.

LT. STEIN: Yes we are. That's exactly what we are planning. That's what the Palace Banquet was – the entire reason I'm stuck in this ridiculous black-op – the Palace Banquet was a well-catered, tasteful affair with a carefully considered guest-list, hand-printed invitations and expensive cake. This mission is a sloppy tongue kiss.

LT. FREUD: Well you can put a woman in uniform but you can't...

COL. JOHNS: This isn't our first date with the target Stein. I think we've earned the right to slip her the tongue.

LT. STEIN: That's just it Colonel. It isn't our first attempt on 'Big 'Stache'. It's the fifth. What will make this attempt work?

COL. JOHNS: Your considerable talent.

LT. STEIN: Well I don't want a suite of flatterers. I want a finished project.

LT. FREUD: You mean a corpse?

LT. STEIN: We don't want the same things Freud. Trust me. If you were running the show we'd still be in Vietnam.

LT. FREUD: Darn tootin'.

COL. JOHNS: You've got a lot to learn Lieutenant Stein. About the Order of Things.

LT. STEIN: What order? What order?

COL. JOHNS: You've got a lot to learn from those bombs of yours Lieutenant. Bombs don't love the plan. Bombs love the enemy.

LT. STEIN: Then you don't need me.

COL. JOHNS: You can see a bomb adapt to the conditions of life in half a second.

LT. STEIN: I quit.

COL. JOHNS: Say that again Lieutenant.

LT. STEIN: I quit.

COL. JOHNS: I'll see you in my office Lieutenant Stein. Now.

10

COL. JOHNS: You think I need you more than you need me?

LT. STEIN: I don't think you need me sir. I think you're stuck with me.

COL. JOHNS: Maybe Lieutenant.

LT. STEIN: It's okay to be against women in the military sir. I am.

COL. JOHNS: I don't object to you Lieutenant, I object to a world too weak to see you in a body bag. I hate the delicate sensibilities of househusbands and working moms who love integration but hate death.

LT. STEIN: I hate death, sir.

COL. JOHNS: Let's change that, shall we?

LT. STEIN: I'm in the habit of hating death sir, and old habits die hard.

COL. JOHNS: I think your mother taught you something and you forgot to forget it.

LT. STEIN: What does my mother have to do with this?

COL. JOHNS: What the child knows is parental detritus. Garbage thought. The leftovers of a mind destroyed by age.

LT. STEIN: I thought you believed in wisdom sir.

COL. JOHNS: I believe in the radiance of my own enlightenment. Your parents? I don't trust them.

LT. STEIN: Tell me sir, what did I forget to forget?

COL. JOHNS: There is no such thing as progress Lieutenant. Only passion, and the lack thereof.

Pause.

LT. STEIN: A marine would never imagine this mission sir. Only a politician would be so undisciplined as to pray for instability.

COL. JOHNS: That isn't your call Lieutenant. You don't have to love the boss, you just have to love thy enemy, and learn to fuck her gently until she ceases to breathe.

Pause.

LT. STEIN: My marine code is governed by morality sir, and a belief in social change.

COL. JOHNS: Are you a pacifist Lieutenant? I am.

LT. STEIN: Negative sir. Even Darwin knew explosions were good.

Pause.

COL. JOHNS: You bomb specialists are all the same. It's all about the Big Bang. If evolution held any water we would have evolved our way out of death! That appears to be the giant pink skid-mark on your doctrine of progress that no one wants to talk about. Wait, let me guess, 'It's coming!' Is that it? We'll 'get there'? 'Sit tight.' 'All things

in good time.' It *is* evolution after all; 'all things...'
including immortality, 'in good time'. You're like Jesus
freaks with your voodoo evolution, I swear to Doug. You
believe in progress? Why? Because the landscape is
dotted with a greater number of incontinent grannies
clutching the handrail so they don't blow away? Fucking
longevity is humanity's botched nose-job. Look at me.
I'm a disgusting mess of expired worm food. I'd take
myself off the shelf if Jesus would let me.

LT. STEIN: Take me off the mission, Colonel.

COL. JOHNS: You don't want me to take you off the
mission.

LT. STEIN: I do Colonel.

COL. JOHNS: I want you to be my ally Lieutenant. I want
to hold on to our lion-hearted women even as the
feminine leaves our body politic. Let it evaporate and
travel with the clouds. Let it rain on darker people in
dryer nations.

LT. STEIN: But I don't think I need your assistance. My
success begs respect. I don't have to say a word.

COL. JOHNS: Let other nations give birth to our children,
Lieutenant. They're good at it.

LT. STEIN: Do I look like I have children?

COL. JOHNS: You don't want off this mission. You've been
detonating phone books and false alarms at Fort
Ticonderoga for the past nine months. No one will touch
you. You're damaged goods. You want perfection? I'm
the only one giving you a chance to fail.

LT. STEIN: I did what responsible soldiers do. I went
public. I never asked for any special favors.

COL. JOHNS: Nobody asks for special favors but when
they are offered it is not customary to refuse.

LT. STEIN: Customary, no. Honorable, yes.

COL. JOHNS: You don't want special treatment. You don't want special assignments. You want to do the work, even when it's dirty. You will defer to the superior wisdom of those in command, perform for the cameras when the cameras need a story. You have no secondary allegiances to your sex or your sisterhood. You hate death and love progress. That's your story?

LT. STEIN: There are worse indignities than explanation.

COL. JOHNS: I know about your past. Your loose lips. Your talent with bombs. That's the best alibi in a military overflowing with toothless volunteers. Honest to God talent kicks dirt all over the footprints of a cum-stained career...

LT. STEIN: I'm a lot of things. But I'm not helpless.

COL. JOHNS: How can I trust a damsel that seems to be in love with her own distress?

LT. STEIN: It seems the more honest I am the less people trust me.

COL. JOHNS: I don't like honesty. I like loyalty.

LT. STEIN: I am loyal to the principle of a public good.

COL. JOHNS: Who are you trying to impress? It's just me here. You want me to shut off the tapes?

LT. STEIN: No sir. I refuse to exist off the record.

Pause.

COL. JOHNS: Okay Lieutenant. Have it your way.

LT. STEIN: You can sign the dismissal papers in the morning.

COL. JOHNS: No Lieutenant. I'm putting you in charge.

LT. STEIN: Sir?

COL. JOHNS: Out with the old. In with the new.

LT. STEIN: Colonel I can't...

COL. JOHNS: I'll let you be the soldier you want to be. I'll follow your lead.

LT. STEIN: Sir. You can't.

COL. JOHNS: I made a promise. I intend to keep it. You're in charge of all operational maneuvers.

LT. STEIN: You think I'm incapable.

COL. JOHNS: Not at all. I'm embracing your remedy to the sickness Lieutenant, don't be ungrateful.

LT. STEIN: Why sir?

COL. JOHNS: Just make sure you keep Freud in line. Understood?

LT. STEIN: Yes Colonel. Thank you Colonel.

11

COL. JOHNS: What do you think about Travis and Emma?

LT. STUDDARD: I don't think about them.

COL. JOHNS: Take a minute then.

LT. STUDDARD: What's to think? I entered the marines so I wouldn't have to think.

COL. JOHNS: Is that it? Has discipline eroded your instinct for gossip? Are you a cyborg? Have we collapsed your capacity for prejudice?

LT. STUDDARD: I have opinions. I just don't remember them.

COL. JOHNS: I need you to be my eyes and ears on this mission.

LT. STUDDARD: Why not refer to the instant replay? (*Indicating the microphone.*)

COL. JOHNS: Look. I've got to misplace my trust somewhere, why can't it be with you?

LT. STUDDARD: Why not consult Lieutenant Freud? He has a gift for interpretation.

COL. JOHNS: Is that what you want? You want me to talk to Freud? Aren't you worried what he'll say about you?

LT. STUDDARD: I don't worry much.

COL. JOHNS: That's good.

Pause.

That's good. I'm going to tell you something. Just you. I'm going to share something with you. You and I will be doing things differently. Travis and Emma, we'll let them continue as before.

LT. STUDDARD: What do you mean?

COL. JOHNS: One must harness their passions, but never let those passions get the best of them. I never doubt the beauty of a target. We need her symmetry in this cock-eyed world of indecision. The brass, they haven't always understood the broader implications of our target's pleasant odor in this world. I'm telling we are going to explore this relationship without necessarily consummating it.

LT. STUDDARD: Sir.

COL. JOHNS: We're not going to kill the target.

Pause.

LT. STUDDARD: So the mission is canceled?

COL. JOHNS: I see no reason to do that.

LT. STUDDARD: Then what are we going to do?

COL. JOHNS: I don't know, flirt a little. Deliver some flowers. It'll be our little secret.

LT. STUDDARD: Why are you telling me this?

COL. JOHNS: I wouldn't tell you Lieutenant, unless I needed some help keeping this thing from getting out of hand.

LT. STUDDARD: What about Stein and Freud?

COL. JOHNS: They will learn to love again. I assume you'll be content to wallow in indifference?

LT. STUDDARD: Not indifference. Neutrality.

COL. JOHNS: Same fuckin' thing.

LT. STUDDARD: Sir, Freud is one thing, Stein is another. Lieutenant Stein is a very capable and driven soldier. Her enthusiasm for the mission is unmatched.

COL. JOHNS: That's why I'm putting her in charge. Her enthusiasm has led to cardinal sin. Stein has fallen in love with the plan. We won't bother to redirect her affections. We'll let her be the public face of our failure. You and I can enjoy the benefits. Does that make sense Lieutenant?

Pause.

LT. STUDDARD: Is this an order?

COL. JOHNS: Yes, it is an order.

LT. STUDDARD: Then it doesn't have to make sense.

12

LT. STEIN: Now you.

LT. FREUD: Now me.

LT. STEIN: Sensitivity to all due weight and effect is necessary.

LT. FREUD: You're ruining my fun.

LT. STEIN: Sorry Travis.

LT. FREUD: What have you got against this mission?

LT. STEIN: Nothing. And everything.

LT. FREUD: Well, let's start with 'nothing'. We'll save 'everything' for the honeymoon.

LT. STEIN: I appreciate the sentiment.

LT. FREUD: Do you? Are you sure you like *to kill things*.

LT. STEIN: I don't like all this poetry. I don't like the bias it conceals. I don't like the loopholes.

LT. FREUD: Those are my favorite parts.

LT. STEIN: I like prose. Simple declarative sentences. Order.

LT. FREUD: You are interfering with my freedom of expression.

LT. STEIN: You like to have fun don't you Travis? Do you think freedom is fun?

LT. FREUD: No I hate it. I want to go to prison.

LT. STEIN: You'd shrivel up and die if there weren't any rules to break.

LT. FREUD: Am I supposed to get down on my knees? Kiss your lines in the sand?

LT. STEIN: We're doing things my way. You should thank me. I'm delivering you from the flaccid and joyless scene into which the advocates of peace would conduct you. If we make it look like an accident we can completely eliminate any fallout or backlash. We'll need to toilet the care-packages and any traceable ballistics or explosive components.

LT. FREUD: Poor tools require better skills Stein.

LT. STEIN: Do you have some of those?

LT. FREUD: You and your fucking 'skills'. Your fucking 'plans'. Why not rush in blind? Justice is blind. What's the worst that could happen?

LT. STEIN: It could stir up the region. Lawlessness. Financial instability.

LT. FREUD: Sounds like freedom to me.

LT. STEIN: Don't play dumb Travis.

LT. FREUD: I don't play dumb.

LT. STEIN: We aren't avenging angels. We're just the foot they lower into the bath.

LT. FREUD: More like the thermometer they shove up the target's ass.

LT. STEIN: Same fucking thing.

Pause.

LT. FREUD: I'm not going to play your game.

LT. STEIN: You will.

LT. FREUD: I won't.

LT. STEIN: You will.

LT. FREUD: I shudder to think what kind of dirty dance you did with daddy to secure this promotion. Did you blackmail him? You find filthy pictures of him nursing a bird back to health?

LT. STEIN: I'm making a point.

LT. FREUD: About what? About freedom? About how much freedom sucks? Aren't we supposed to be fighting oppression?

LT. STEIN: Who got you so excited about fighting oppression? You're a fucking *marine*. You signed up for a job where your boss can force you to do *push-ups.* You *love* oppression.

LT. FREUD: Yeah, but I *signed up* for it.

LT. STEIN: Is that what we do? Invade dirt-farms in unpronounceable corners of the world so the citizenry might one day *elect* to discipline itself? There's no point.

LT. FREUD: I don't like elections. I like intervention.

LT. STEIN: Why not skip the middle-man?

LT. FREUD: Because. Because then the starving-class would never know the Judeo-christian ecstasy of a diet-regime. The limbless, they'd miss out on decades of aerobics. The impoverished radicals, they'd never know the joy of wasting a privilege. True freedom is a performance of waste. Sanctioned by zealots and handsome free radicals. You're just a marine. Obsessed with discipline. Driven by a compulsion to share.

LT. STEIN: And you're a cliché.

LT. FREUD: What are you? A hooker with a heart of gold? Are you a cyborg struggling to let the human side take over?

LT. STEIN: There are two methods of removing our malignant opposition. The one: by extinguishing the liberty which is essential to its existence. The other: by giving to all peoples the same opinions, the same passions, and the same interests. I'm ambitious. I want both. I want rules and regulations. I want patterns of behavior. I want lexicons and manuals. There is no emotion Freud. Only a plan. A set of predictions. The conditions. No evil. Just our hypothesis. The test, and the results.

LT. FREUD: Well you're new school. I don't like your game. It doesn't make me feel good. I don't care if everything lines up. I'm old school. You want to be part

of an occupying army? With a benevolent philosophy?
Huh? Correcting the chaos and teaching them how to
fucking recycle? Well I don't want to recycle. I don't
want to keep our planet *green*. I want to live on a fragile
planet. I want to fuck on the verge of extinction.

13

COL. JOHNS: Finally we make the transition from ground
to sky. American culture comes off like wet corduroys
on a hot day doesn't it kids?

LT. STEIN: Is that a good thing?

LT. FREUD: I can't wait to go native.

LT. STEIN: How long until the drop?

COL. JOHNS: It's surprisingly hard on the ankles.

LT. FREUD: Your ankles.

COL. JOHNS: I'm young at heart.

LT. STEIN: Studdard, we're going to go over the itinerary.

LT. FREUD: Worst thing about drops is trees. I don't see
any trees.

LT. STEIN: Studdard!

LT. STUDDARD: Emma, I'm not going over it again.

LT. STEIN: We aren't going to play this by ear. Let's review
the procedure.

COL. JOHNS: I think everyone knows their role
Lieutenant Stein.

LT. STEIN: I want to minimize the need for improvisation.

LT. STUDDARD: We're going to rendezvous with land
support at 2300 hours.

LT. STEIN: Where?

LT. STUDDARD: Half mile from the drop zone.

COL. JOHNS: Everything looks so calm and democratic from this height. Disappointment is in the details, I'll tell you. That's what my father said.

LT. STUDDARD: We'll be riding in the back of civilian truck to grid point E12 which is approximately two miles from the hot spot.

LT. STEIN: I'm telling you right now: We aren't using that driver.

LT. STUDDARD: The driver is going to get us through two checkpoints.

LT. FREUD: Fuck him. I'm clipping that fool. I'll drive the fucking truck.

LT. STEIN: We'll leave the driver at the checkpoint.

LT. STUDDARD: Colonel?

COL. JOHNS: Look at it! It could be Tijuana from up here.

LT. FREUD: It could be Tijuana from down there.

LT. STUDDARD: Are you going to authorize those changes to the...

LT. STEIN: I don't need to authorize those orders Lieutenant Studdard. I just need to say them.

LT. FREUD: We'll drive around the goddam checkpoints Harpo, it's the fucking desert.

LT. STUDDARD: Travis, that'll cost us two hours.

LT. FREUD: I'm superstitious.

COL. JOHNS: Hey, I haven't washed this uniform in six years.

LT. STEIN: We won't be sidetracked by any improvisational flourish or superstitious hokey-pokey.

COL. JOHNS: You mean hanky-panky.

LT. STUDDARD: You'll regret the loss of my trust Emma.

LT. FREUD: Shouldn't you be tongue-kissing your walkie-talkie?

LT. STEIN: Can it. Both of you can it.

COL. JOHNS: Can it!

LT. STUDDARD: Colonel?

COL. JOHNS: You can it! Everyone can it! Everyone be silent. Enjoy the delicate sounds of destiny.

LT. FREUD: I might be a prisoner of conscience, but there is still enough room in here (*Indicating his head.*) for blood lust and a little common sense.

LT. STUDDARD: It isn't common sense if you're the only one who thinks so.

COL. JOHNS: Can it! Fucking CAN IT! Now can't you two see that you're in love with each other? We can't have that. What about 'The Bearded Lady'? What is she supposed to do? What about the lonely target? Who will keep her warm at night with you two wasting all this heat on each other?

LT. STEIN: I was just going to go over that. Our man will deliver us to the hot spot. Lieutenant Freud will not be clipping the driver.

LT. FREUD: Can I shave his mustache?

LT. STEIN: The Colonel and Lieutenant Studdard will be positioned outside the perimeter wall of the compound. When Studdard has disabled the security system and cut the phones, myself and Lieutenant Freud will enter mansion and do the deed. Nothing too difficult.

COL. JOHNS: If there are any problems we will simply abort the mission.

LT. STEIN: We aren't aborting anything.

LT. FREUD: Hold on, we aren't aborting anything.

LT. STEIN: I've got it.

LT. STUDDARD: We're two minutes from the drop.

LT. STEIN: All right Freud. This is your chance to clean up that spotty combat record.

LT. FREUD: Those spots are blood.

COL. JOHNS: Your body should be manipulated by authority, rather than imbued with animal spirits.

LT. FREUD: Really? Is that true? Stein?

LT. STEIN: I don't know Travis.

LT. FREUD: Let me explain something: As long as I'm the trigger man on this mission I'll expect oodles and oodles of room to breathe for every petty superstition, gut feeling, sixth sense, –

COL. JOHNS: Calm down Freud.

LT. FREUD: – every facial tic, muscle spasm, and bathroom break will be lovingly accommodated by you, and you, and definitely you.

LT. STEIN: All right Travis.

LT. FREUD: Unless you want to pull the trigger? You want that responsibility?

LT. STUDDARD: I would cherish that responsibility.

LT. FREUD: Fine! It's yours!

LT. STEIN: Try to think about the big picture Freud.

COL. JOHNS: That's modern romance.

LT. FREUD: Take it, you're the triggerman now!

LT. STEIN: Hey, are you insane? Are you suffering from...

LT. FREUD: I'm suffering. Certainly suffering. From a case of bad faith and menstrual cramps. I'm suffering by proximity.

LT. STUDDARD: Grow up Travis.

LT. FREUD: AH! Give me your job Harpo, instead of push-ups I'll cultivate moral superiority.

LT. STUDDARD: I was born with that.

LT. FREUD: You're cruising for a bruising.

LT. STEIN: I hope you put that parachute on upside down.

COL. JOHNS: Leave your memories behind. We need to travel light.

LT. STEIN: Should I leave my brain behind?

LT. FREUD: You'll definitely have more fun.

COL. JOHNS: Just bring your heart. That's the muscle that pulls the trigger.

14

The desert. LT. STEIN and LT. FREUD are in a different location than COL. JOHNS and LT. STUDDARD. They are communicating by radio.

LT. STEIN: We're in position Colonel.

LT. STUDDARD: Colonel, they are in position.

COL. JOHNS: Hold position.

LT. STUDDARD: Hold position Stein.

LT. STEIN: We're holding.

COL. JOHNS: We haven't been detected?

LT. STUDDARD: Negative sir. I'm hearing every land and mobile line. There is no activity.

LT. FREUD: You know, if this were a proper sniper mission I'd have a nest.

LT. STUDDARD: Keep this line clear Lieutenant Freud.

LT. FREUD: Christ.

LT. STUDDARD: Colonel. They are in position to advance.

COL. JOHNS: Do they still have visual contact?

LT. STUDDARD: Lieutenant Stein, I'm going to send a visual signal, it should register on your northwest horizon line. Come back.

LT. STEIN: I'm waiting Lieutenant.

LT. STUDDARD: That's ABC, 123, over.

LT. FREUD: What are we waiting for?

LT. STEIN: Studdard is sending a visual signal.

LT. STUDDARD: Lieutenant?

LT. STEIN: Affirmative. I'm reading ABC123 in the my northwest corner.

LT. STUDDARD: Affirmative Colonel. I'm placing them about two miles from our location.

LT. FREUD: Are we advancing?

COL. JOHNS: What time is it?

LT. STUDDARD: Sir, it is four-thirty-five a.m. local time.

COL. JOHNS: I should have let Freud drive around those checkpoints. We should be ten miles lost by now.

LT. STUDDARD: They are positioned perfectly Colonel.

COL. JOHNS: Do you know why Lieutenant Freud is on this mission?

LT. STEIN: Something is wrong.

LT. FREUD: Is he responding?

COL. JOHNS: 'Cause he's a goddam screw-up. He is ranked last among marine snipers. How do you like that?

LT. STUDDARD: What about Emma?

COL. JOHNS: Lieutenant Stein's career was over nine months ago. Can we stall them any longer?

LT. STUDDARD: Colonel, we're actually ahead of schedule.

COL. JOHNS: Ask them if they can see the mansion?

LT. STUDDARD: Lieutenant Stein, can you see the mansion?

LT. STEIN: Affirmative Lieutenant. We could see the mansion from our previous position.

LT. STUDDARD: Colonel they can still see the mansion.

COL. JOHNS: No obstructions?

LT. FREUD: Are we going or what? I can see three potential targets from here.

LT. STUDDARD: Lieutenant is your view still unobstructed?

LT. FREUD: Tell me what he's saying. Harpo, come back.

LT. STEIN: Harpo, what the fuck is going on?

LT. FREUD: Are they giving an order? What's the order?

LT. STUDDARD: Lieutenant, is your view unobstructed? Come back.

LT. STEIN: He is asking if our view is still unobstructed?

LT. FREUD: No, there's a redwood forest in the way. Permission to burn it down?

LT. STUDDARD: Come back.

LT. STEIN: Lieutenant, there are no obstructions. Permission to advance?

LT. STUDDARD: Their view is unobstructed sir.

COL. JOHNS: Alright, is Freud in position to eliminate the perimeter guards?

LT. STUDDARD: Lieutenant Freud. Come back.

LT. FREUD: What is it Harpo?

LT. STUDDARD: Can you execute movement two?

LT. FREUD: Affirmative, I just need to use two bursts.

LT. STUDDARD: He says he needs two bursts.

COL. JOHNS: Two bursts? Why?

LT. STUDDARD: Lieutenant Freud, hold. Movement two should be a single burst, six seconds.

LT. STEIN: What is it?

LT. FREUD: I need to use two bursts.

LT. STEIN: Okay.

LT. FREUD: Movement two is one burst.

LT. STEIN: I can authorize two bursts.

LT. STUDDARD: Lieutenant Freud, movement two should be a single burst...

COL. JOHNS: This is it. We can pull them out.

LT. FREUD: Harpo, I've been sitting here for ten minutes. A single burst will put down guards one and two but most likely put our third man on the run. We can't risk a fast-moving target at this distance. He could duck behind that retaining wall and trigger an alarm.

LT. STUDDARD: He says a single burst will put man three on the run.

COL. JOHNS: Why would two bursts fix that problem?

LT. STEIN: Studdard, we need to move NOW. I can authorize two bursts.

LT. STUDDARD: Lieutenant Freud, why would two burst fix that problem?

LT. FREUD: Fuck this. I'm taking out the perimeter guards.

LT. STEIN: Just one second Travis...

LT. FREUD: Harpo, I'm taking my shots now.

LT. STUDDARD: You hold on Freud.

LT. STEIN: Just let me authorize the change in procedure.

LT. FREUD: Cover your ears.

LT. STEIN: Harpo, Harpo I'm authorizing two bursts.

LT. STUDDARD: Shit, he's taking the shot.

COL. JOHNS: Christ. Put her on my line.

LT. STUDDARD: Emma, I'm transferring you directly to Colonel...

LT. FREUD fires.

LT. STEIN: Shit Travis shit shit...

COL. JOHNS: Emma what the fuck are you...

LT. FREUD fires.

LT. FREUD: Man three rounding the corner.

COL. JOHNS: Hold fire Lieutenant. Now.

LT. STEIN: Colonel the movement is being executed.

LT. FREUD: Wait. Wait. Wait.

LT. STEIN: Take him out Freud.

COL. JOHNS: Lieutenant Stein, this isn't the plan.

LT. STEIN: Travis take the shot now he's about to –

LT. FREUD fires.

COL. JOHNS: Lieutenant Stein, what is going on?

LT. FREUD: Can you authorize all my maneuvers from now on?

LT. STEIN: Colonel with all due respect we are completing this mission.

COL. JOHNS: What happened to the plan Lieutenant?

LT. STEIN: Colonel, we can't allow our passions to dilute our focus.

LT. FREUD: You see that? Fucking gross.

COL. JOHNS: Take me off this line.

LT. STUDDARD: Emma, you're back on line with me.

COL. JOHNS: Tell them to hold position.

LT. STUDDARD: Hold position Emma.

LT. STEIN: Holding.

COL. JOHNS: It wasn't supposed to get this far. Oh Jesus. How did we get so close. This isn't where we want to be. FUCK FUCK FUCK FUCK.

LT. STUDDARD: Colonel, movement three puts them inside the mansion.

LT. FREUD: Do you feel that Emma? Those guys just became three of my best friends.

LT. STEIN: Can you get us inside the mansion?

LT. FREUD: Can you feel how much sense the world is making all of sudden?

LT. STUDDARD: It's Freud Colonel.

LT. STEIN: We are going to finish what we started. We are going to execute this plan.

COL. JOHNS: I guess that's love for you. Goddamit.

LT. STEIN: Harpo, we need to execute movement three right now.

LT. FREUD: Listen to you.

LT. STEIN: Shut the fuck up Travis.

LT. FREUD: Begging for permission to exist.

LT. STEIN: Harpo, we need to advance right now.

COL. JOHNS: Terribly good excuse to bump heads.

LT. FREUD: I feel sorry for you.

LT. STUDDARD: Colonel they aren't going to hold position.

COL. JOHNS: An index of this world's persistent delusion.

LT. STUDDARD: Colonel?

COL. JOHNS: Thank god we've still got Lieutenant Freud.

LT. STEIN: Harpo, we are executing movement three right now.

LT. STUDDARD: Negative Emma. Wait for our signal. Negative negative. Wait for confirmation.

LT. STEIN: You cover me Freud.

LT. STEIN and LT. FREUD have entered the mansion.

LT. FREUD: Fuck this I'm going upstairs.

LT. STEIN: We don't have time Travis. I need to rig the instrument.

LT. FREUD: We need visual confirmation.

LT. STEIN: Travis YOU NEED TO STAY. The bomb will take care of everything.

LT. FREUD: You don't know how to have any fun.

LT. STUDDARD: Colonel she's going to set the instrument.

LT. FREUD: Are you as turned on as I am right now?

COL. JOHNS: Ten centuries won't teach us that love is to be avoided at all costs.

LT. STUDDARD: Colonel that bomb will level the entire building.

LT. STEIN: Harpo, I'm ready to set the instrument.

Pause.

LT. STUDDARD: Colonel she's in position. She's waiting for the order.

COL. JOHNS: FUCK FUCK. What happens if she sets that bomb?

LT. STUDDARD: Colonel 'Big 'Stache' is in the building. If she sets the bomb the target will be eliminated.

LT. STEIN: This is how it works Travis. This is how you accomplish something.

COL. JOHNS: I can't let her set that bomb Harpo.

LT. STUDDARD: What's the order Colonel?

LT. STEIN: I'm waiting for your order Colonel.

COL. JOHNS: I can't let her finish this mission Harpo. We need the target more than we need her.

LT. STUDDARD: Colonel.

COL. JOHNS: It isn't pretty, Harpo. You understand. Don't you? No more targets, no more history.

LT. STUDDARD: I understand.

COL. JOHNS: It didn't have to be this way. She's a good soldier. It's nothing personal.

LT. STUDDARD: It's nothing personal.

COL. JOHNS: She's good at what she does.

LT. STEIN: Harpo, I'm ready to set the bomb. I'm waiting for your order.

COL. JOHNS: Use Freud.

LT. STUDDARD: Should we try to pull them out?

COL. JOHNS: She won't pull out Harpo. Trust me. Use Freud. Use Freud.

LT. STUDDARD radios LT. FREUD privately.

LT. STUDDARD: Lieutenant Freud.

LT. FREUD: What is it Harpo?

Pause.

LT. STUDDARD: There has been a change of plans.

LT. FREUD: Fuck your plans.

LT. STEIN: Quiet Freud.

LT. STUDDARD: Are you reading me Lieutenant Freud?

LT. STEIN: For a sniper you're not very precise.

LT. FREUD: I just fire at the shades of gray.

LT. STUDDARD: Travis, the target has changed.

Pause.

We're going to leave Emma there.

Pause.

That's the new plan.

Pause.

Lieutenant Freud, we don't want Emma to finish that bomb.

Pause.

LT. FREUD: What is this?

COL. JOHNS: She's the only target he's going to get.

LT. STUDDARD: Lieutenant, she is the only target you're going to get.

Pause.

Lieutenant, if you disobey this order it will be the last one you receive.

LT. STEIN: Progress is the only thing worth believing in Travis. This is what a good job looks like.

LT. FREUD: What does it look like Emma?

LT. STEIN: Like this. Like a perfect little bomb.

LT. FREUD: I don't know. I like to see the whites of her eyes.

LT. FREUD points his gun at LT. STEIN'S head. She doesn't see what he is doing.

LT. STEIN: Of course. You're a hopeless romantic.

LT. FREUD: I can't afford to be picky.

LT. STEIN: No. You're passionate.

LT. FREUD: Lieutenant Stein, would you like to have nine of my babies?

LT. STEIN: Quiet now Travis. 'The Bearded Lady' might hear you.

LT. FREUD: How about just one?

LT. STEIN: God, I love bombs.

15

The remaining dialogue is a recording played through the speakers. It is LT. STUDDARD'S 'official record'.

LT. STUDDARD: Lieutenant Freud? Lieutenant Freud?

LT. FREUD: It's done Harpo.

COL. JOHNS: Let's get him out of there.

LT. FREUD: Am I leaving her here?

COL. JOHNS: Leave her.

LT. STUDDARD: Leave her there Lieutenant.

LT. FREUD: What about 'Big 'Stache'?

COL. JOHNS: You've had your fun Lieutenant. Come back.

LT. FREUD: What about the official record?

LT. STUDDARD: I've seen worse.

LT. FREUD: Should I pin a medal on her chest now? Or are we waiting for the body to come home?

COL. JOHNS: Turn off the tape Harpo.

LT. FREUD: Lucky bitch.

LT. STUDDARD: Language.

LT. FREUD: You've seen worse.

COL. JOHNS: Turn off the tape Harpo.

Pause.

Turn off the goddam tape, n–

The recording cuts out.

End